"What insights pack the pages of Steve .... _Windows to the_ _Father's Heart!_ More than once I had to stop and think about the beauty of what I was reading. It became a study manual for me to look deeper through the windows of our Father's heart! What I saw was breathtaking. What I learned is eternal. You will be captivated by the short but powerful chapters of Steve's book. It's written from the heart of a missionary, a passionate follower of Jesus, and a true teacher. Get ready for a feast. The relationship this author has with the Father of Glory comes through each page. Keep this book with you and go through it more than once. Oh, and make sure you get a copy for your pastor or a friend; they will thank you for it!"

Dr. Brian Simmons
Stairway Ministries
The Passion Translation Project

"Here is a collection of lessons learned by a man who is pursuing God with all his heart. _Windows to the Father's Heart_ is a manual on how to build a tomorrow in God and which building materials to use. We all have our ideas of what is important and sometimes end up building lives that even we don't want to live in. Steve Trullinger is helping us avoid that mistake by nicely laying out a path to love mercy, do justly, and walk humbly with our God. I highly recommend _Windows to the Father's Heart_ to anyone wanting to check themselves as they build a life in honor of our Father."

Danny Silk
Author of _Culture of Honor: Sustaining a Supernatural Environment;_
Loving Our Kids On Purpose: Making a Heart-to-Heart Connection;
Powerful & Free; and _Keep Your Love On! Connection, Communication, &_
Boundaries

"God designed the family to be a safe, nurturing place where a child can grow into their true identity and purpose. Father interactions are crucial to this development. But because of a lack of fatherhood, many struggle with issues in their adult life. These are the issues Steve Trullinger deals with as he masterfully writes _Windows to the Father's Heart._ Steve shares deep revelation and insights that will heal the heart and bring you into a glorious relationship, not just with Jesus and Holy Spirit but also with your amazing heavenly Father. The Father wants you to know Him. This book will bring you into a deeper intimacy with your heavenly Father and in the process heal you and cause you to become everything God has designed and destined you to be. I know you will love reading it!"

Matt Sorger
Author, International Speaker, Healing and Prophetic Minister
Matt Sorger Ministries

"Steve Trullinger created a book that will build your identity as you look through God the Father's eyes. It creates and promotes healthy understanding of your position to the Father and His to you. Although deeply theological and inspirational, I encourage the reader to use it as a devotional and spend time thinking about the different 'windows' that are taught as you grasp who your heavenly Abba is. This book teaches how to create that deep, meaningful connection for which God paid the price, the one you have always dreamed you could have."

Shawn Bolz
Author of *Translating God: Hearing God's Voice for Yourself and the World Around You; Growing Up with God: Everyday Adventures of Hearing God's Voice;* and *Keys to Heaven's Economy*
www.bolzministries.com

"Wow, wow, wow! What a great book! I couldn't put it down. Steve is a lover of God's presence. I already knew that. What I didn't know is that he has a deep knowledge of our Father's heart. *Windows to the Father's Heart* took me on a journey, seeing and experiencing facets of Abba Father's nature that deeply moved me. As I read this book, mostly in an airport on a long layover, I was drawn into a transcendent and holy realm of gratitude and worship. That's pretty amazing in an airport! Without exaggeration, this is one of the most refreshing reads I've had in years. Steve's open and vulnerable style drew me right in and I couldn't put it down."

Charles Stock
Senior Leader, Life Center Ministries, Harrisburg, Pennsylvania
Founder of Clear River Network

"Steve Trullinger has written an excellent book on *Windows to the Father's Heart*. It is a good story about God the Father's heart. I really like the windows the author helps us peek through to see the Father's heart. One of my favorite windows to peek through was the window of the Father's affection. The book talks about the Father kissing us from heaven. Even daily kisses! Many people see God as far away and distant emotionally. Steve paints a great picture of God's desire for us to experience and feel His love. God is love! As you look through these windows and read the Scriptures within this book, you will be transformed. The real life illustrations and experiences will draw you into the Father's presence. Enjoy the Father's love—His windows are open."

Dr. Dan Hammer
Senior Pastor, Sonrise Christian Center
President, Seattle Bible College

"Through Christ Jesus we have received the spirit of adoption and we have been grafted into the greatest family ever with the best Father ever. He really is a good, good Father! Steve Trullinger opens up *Windows to the Father's Heart* so we can really see who He is and who we can become in Him. Whether you are a new believer in Jesus or been around for a while, you will benefit from the writings of this dear man of God."

James W. Goll
Cofounder of God Encounters Ministries
International Director of Prayer Storm
International Best-selling Author of over 25 books. They include *The Lost Art of Intercession, The Seer, Dream Language, The Coming Israel Awakening,* and many others.

WINDOWS

Father's Heart
to the

Exploring the Most Fascinating Place in the Universe

STEVE TRULLINGER

5 Fold Media
Visit us at www.5foldmedia.com

Windows to the Father's Heart: Exploring the Most Fascinating Place in the Universe
Copyright 2017 by Steve Trullinger
Published by 5 Fold Media, LLC
www.5foldmedia.com

ISBN: 978-1-942056-42-3

Library of Congress Control Number: 2017936548

Dedication

This book is dedicated to the memory of my father, Lawrence Eugene Trullinger, who blessed my boyhood with numerous examples of love and quality time invested as father with son.

I bless my children, grandchildren, and great-grandchildren (and their entire progeny) with the joy of knowing Abba so intimately that they will share in His vision of succeeding generations of our family as interwoven relationships that span space and time and find their eternal fulfillment deep in the heart of their Abba.

I also bless those of my forefathers who have rejoined the family of God with the exquisite joy of seeing their legacy rooted and enlarged in the heart of Abba even as they continue to cheer us on. I can see that joy manifested in the warmed heart of the Father of us all.

Acknowledgments

Several beloved friends and advisors have encouraged me to share the insights and revelations that have blessed me over the years as Abba has responded to my desire to know Him better. These prods to write have spanned quite a spectrum of forcefulness, from the gentlest of nudges to outright arm-twisting, and I am so very grateful for all of them! Notable among these "prod-meisters" are Ché Ahn, Chad Dedmon, John Johnson, Steve Lemme, Mark Mitchell, Laurie Nickisch, and Brian Simmons, as well as many of my spiritual sons and daughters around the globe. The support of these champions of the revelation of Abba's love has been a wonderful blessing to me, and now also to the many readers who will be peering deeper into the most fascinating place in the universe.

I'm also very blessed because of the heart investments by Andy and Cathy Sanders and their staff at 5 Fold Media. Their desire to equip the body of Christ by helping to shepherd the writings of Christian authors has been quite refreshing to me and a source of encouragement throughout the publishing process.

Contents

Foreword

I have known Steve Trullinger for a number of years; in fact, he is a member of an apostolic network and was commissioned as an apostle of Harvest International Ministry (H.I.M), of which I am the president and founder. Steve truly demonstrates and imparts the Father's heart wherever he goes. Whether he is training a missions team; traveling the nations speaking, empowering, and raising up spiritual sons and daughters; or leading his own ministry, The Father's Touch, Steve's life has been infused with a very powerful revelation about the love of the Father and His purpose for each and every one of us. This is why I am so excited about this timely book by Steve, *Windows to the Father's Heart.*

In Ephesians 1:17-19, the apostle Paul prayed for the church—that we would know God, that our very hearts and understanding would be enlightened to receive who He is and in turn know who we are. There is nothing more profound than knowing God and being known by Him. It is from Steve's own encounters with the love of God and inquisitiveness with the Holy Spirit that *Windows to the Father's Heart* presents simple and straightforward questions from the perspective of a son or daughter to their Father, who just so happens to be the best Dad in the whole world.

As Steve answers each question about the heart, character, and beautiful intentions of our Father toward us with the replies he himself received from the Lord, this book becomes a powerful invitation for each of us to have encounters with the Godhead that will reveal the Father's heart to us more and more. In this place of God-discovery, self-discovery (truly recognizing our identity as sons and daughters of God) and transformation is inevitable.

Steve's hunger for God is palpable and even more so his desire for God's children to have the truth of their adoption in Christ and their value and delight to the Father be settled in their hearts. *Windows to the Father's Heart* is a refreshing, biblically-based book that reminds us of the love of God that is so very high, deep, wide, and long (Ephesians 3:17-19) that it has the power to heal, deliver, set free, and change us from the inside out. In all that Steve accomplishes through this book, the most powerful is that it encourages you to go deeper into the Father's heart and seek an encounter with Him yourself that will reveal the place in His heart that is shaped just like you.

Dr. Ché Ahn
President, Harvest International Ministry Founding Pastor, HROCK Church, Pasadena, California
International Chancellor, Wagner Leadership Institute

Introduction

"God, why couldn't I get out of my chair?"

I kept asking this question over and over again for an *entire week* in February of 1992. No, I wasn't paralyzed, at least not more than a few minutes near the end of the Sunday morning service on February 16 at Hope Chapel in Hermosa Beach, California.

I was desperate to find a way to gain a moral foundation in my life, to find a way out of the self-centeredness that was causing pain and suffering in the lives of some of my loved ones. After a handful of visits to a church recommended by a friend of mine, I found this particular service different from the others. This time the pastor extended an invitation at the end of the service to those who wanted to receive forgiveness for their sins and begin a brand-new life in surrender to Jesus as their Savior and Lord.

That was exactly what I wanted, exactly what I sought. I had heard the gospel message more than once during my few visits and something powerful was stirring inside of me. I was ready to say "Yes!" to Jesus. The pastor repeated the invitation as a few people rose from their seats and made their way to the altar to surrender their lives to Christ and make a public profession of faith in His death and resurrection for their sake.

I thought I was ready to join them at the altar. *But I couldn't get out of my chair.* Several people had assembled in front, and the pastor said again, "I know there is still someone else among you who would like to come forward. Please come now." I tried to rise, but it felt like something was holding me down in my chair. I simply couldn't move.

I was not afraid to get up in front of people—I already had a long career of teaching and experience in speaking before crowds. I knew this was supposed to be a precious personal moment of surrender to God's care, not dependent on what other people might think of me. *But I couldn't get out of my chair.*

The pastor finally gave up with further invitation, and led the people at the altar in their prayer of surrender. The whole congregation cheered in approval and great joy. I was jealous. There I sat, "glued" to my chair and mystified by my inaction. As the pastor dismissed the congregation with a blessing, I was finally able to stand along with everyone else and exit with all the happy people.[1]

But it was too late—I had missed the moment of opportunity. My temporary "paralysis" had ruined my day, and maybe my chance at a new life. What if I died that night in my sin? I was frightened by that prospect, one that I had been confronted with more than once in the past few weeks. If the pastor had another invitation at a future service, would I still be glued to my seat? How many chances would come my way? I kept asking, *"God, why couldn't I get out of my chair?"*

I kept asking that question, several times per day, during the entire next week. The next Saturday night (February 22), I was still mystified and frightened. I thought, *Tomorrow morning I will be at the church service; what if the pastor has one of those "invitation things" and I still can't get out of my chair? How many chances will I get?* I shuddered at the thought of missing another opportunity. *"God, why couldn't I get out of my chair?"*

I was desperate to know the answer. If only I knew the reason, maybe I could do something about it. I got down on my knees alone in

---

1. When I left the sanctuary and picked up my ten-year-old son, Joseph, from children's church, I noticed he had bloodshot eyes and tear tracks running down his cheeks. I asked, "What's wrong, son?" He said, "Nothing's wrong, Dad. I just gave my life to Jesus." I was glad for him, and jealous at the same time. I asked him to tell me what it was like, and all he could do was cry with joy. That made my own passion for salvation even more intense.

my apartment in Redondo Beach and cried out to God, this time in tears, *"God, why couldn't I get out of my chair?"* Now, finally, He answered me. I heard an audible (to me at least) voice say, "Because you don't feel worthy." Somehow, I knew it was Father God speaking, and He let me ponder that statement. I agreed. It was true. I felt so unworthy to be in God's family; it was horrible to feel so disqualified.

A few moments went by as I agonized over my unworthiness, and then He spoke again, "Son, nobody is worthy." In a heartbeat, the very best heartbeat I ever experienced, I knew what He meant. Somehow I now knew that I was being offered a free gift, a gift I could not earn. A gift for which I could not qualify. A gift that had been paid for by Jesus. I sobbed in surrender to this truth for a long time that night.

Asking for an "Invitation Thing"

The next morning, I could hardly wait to get to the first service at the church. I arrived several minutes early. The pastor was greeting people on their way into the sanctuary, and I gobbled up some of his time to share my experience during the service the prior Sunday, my desperate wrestle during the ensuing week, and my conversation with Father God the night before. I looked my pastor in the eye and asked, "So, do you think you could have one of those 'invitation things' today?"

I thought I had to respond to the "invitation thing" in order to be saved. I didn't realize that I had actually received my salvation the night before, in tearful realization of the truth and my subsequent surrender to the Truth. Even though the pastor protested a little, saying he normally didn't "plan" those invitations, I realized later that he was just "testing" my sincerity. I walked into the sanctuary thinking, *What a jerk. He didn't seem that excited about my plea. But sooner or later, he is going to have another one of those "invitation things," and I'm going to be here at every service* [six per weekend] *until he does. I'm not missing the very next opportunity to get saved.*

Of course he had an "invitation thing" at the end of the service. I was out of my chair in an instant, rushing to the altar to be the first to give my life to Jesus that morning. I was in such a hurry that I think I must have left shoe marks on the thighs of the people in my row between my chair and the aisle. (I don't think they held that against me.)

I was on cloud ninety-nine as I left that morning, only to return that same evening for the bimonthly baptism service that "just happened" to be scheduled for that night. Several hundred people cheered when I gave my testimony and was baptized into my new life with the resurrected Jesus. I now belonged to my new family. My former unworthiness was now trumped by the sacrifice of the Worthy One.

My salvation, in fact, had been accomplished the night before, as I mentioned, when I surrendered to the loving ministry of the Father's voice speaking to my heart. I was saved because of the audible voice of my Father showing me that a gift was being freely offered to me— "prepaid." Abba had opened a "window of grace" into His heart for me to see the overwhelming love that provided for my salvation. Something began burning in me that night, a yearning to know this loving heart better.

Thus began my frequent prayer all these years since February 22, 1992:

"Daddy, show me more of Your heart."

This fervent prayer (in some form) has been cried countless times, as believers everywhere and in every age have expressed their desire to know Him more. This reflects a *universal* hunger to know Abba's heart and to have a deepening relationship with Him. A huge part of our blessing from heaven is our invitation to embark on an exquisite, eternal exploration of the infinite heart of our Father.

What about Dad?

Let me suggest an experiment, one that helps reveal the purpose for this book. Try asking a few of your Christian friends to describe their relationship with Jesus. Most likely, they will talk for quite a long time as they relate experiences, encounters, conversations, and shared moments with the Lover of their souls. You will no doubt rejoice in the stories they tell, the testimonies they share with you, and the deep and powerful impact their relationship with Jesus has had on their lives.

Introduction

Next, ask those same friends to describe their relationship with the Holy Spirit. Again, most of them will be able, and delighted, to relate experiences, encounters, conversations, and shared moments with their Counselor, their Comforter, the Seal of their redemption, their Power Source. Once again, you will likely be able to rejoice for quite a while as they continue to share with you the amazing facets of their relationship with the Whisperer.

Finally, finish your experiment by asking those same friends to describe their relationship with Abba, their Father. If your experiment follows along the same lines as my own, I think you will find that only a few of your friends will be able to talk for more than fifteen seconds about their relationship with their heavenly Father. Typical responses are the listing of His attributes such as His omnipresence, omniscience, omnipotence, goodness, holiness, and so on, but you probably won't hear much regarding actual conversations, enjoyable joint experiences, and shared moments of intimacy. In fact, if your friends talk for more than fifteen seconds, they may well steer their description back to Jesus or the Holy Spirit.

My last question for friends in the experiment is usually along this line:

"But what about Dad?"

In other words, what do you talk about with Him? What kind of "walks" do you take together? What moves His heart about your life? Do you know His favorite things? Do you know where His "tickle spots" are?

To be sure, there are many Christians who can give extensive answers to these sorts of questions concerning Abba, but there are far more who cannot. This is not a condemnation by any means, but simply an observation of a deep need in many believers to know Abba Father on a much more intimate level. Put another way, loving and satisfying relationships (for example, those characterized by *intimacy*) between Father and His children are tantalizingly close, but for many believers they seem afar off.

The Joy Set before Jesus

Many years ago, I attended a class for men being taught by a pastor who was well respected in our community. At a particular point in the discussion, our attention was focused on this passage from Scripture:

> *Fixing our eyes on Jesus, the author and perfecter of faith, who for the joy set before Him endured the cross, despising the shame, and has sat down at the right hand of the throne of God* (Hebrews 12:2 NASB).

One of the men asked the pastor this question: "What was the joy set before Jesus?"

The pastor offered his opinion: "Jesus looked forward to being reunited with His Father."

That answer didn't sit well with me because it implied that Jesus' focus was on Himself and that was surely not in His nature; I was disturbed in my spirit as I pondered the real reason for Jesus' imminent joy. After the class, I approached the pastor with another interpretation (which he welcomed and agreed with, by the way), one that was based on the *others-focus* of the Lover of our souls. I felt sure that the joy set before Jesus stemmed from His knowledge that by enduring the cross He would pave the way for all of us to have the *same kind of relationship* with the Father that He enjoyed.

Jesus and the Father both enjoy a relationship characterized by deep, intimate knowledge of one another, the *yada*[2] of the Hebrew language. They delight in each other, as Father and Son, as friends, as lovers of one another, as eternal companions and workmates, and so on. This relationship is the very best example of the destiny that continues to unfold for you and me with our Abba.

Jesus sacrificed on our behalf so that we could enjoy the beautiful relationship predestined[3] for us with Abba. It is sobering to realize that

---

2. James Strong, *The New Strong's Exhaustive Concordance of the Bible*, s.v. "yada," H3045, https://www.blueletterbible.org.

3. See Romans 8:29.

Introduction

if we don't pursue the deepening of our relationship with our Father, there is sadness in the heart of Jesus because He yearns so strongly for us to enjoy what He has. Put more positively, we have an invitation from the triune Godhead to know our Father better. The apostle Paul prayed this very blessing for the saints:

> I keep asking that the God of our Lord Jesus Christ, the glorious Father, may give you the Spirit of wisdom and revelation, so that you may know him better (Ephesians 1:17).

This is also my prayer for you.

Windows to the Father's Heart

In February 2014, I was asked to speak on the Father's heart to a congregation in Langley, British Columbia. My arm did not need to be "twisted" for me to accept this wonderful invitation to share a sample of some of the love expressions I had "seen" in the Father's heart as He continued to answer the frequent prayer I mentioned above: *"Daddy, show me more of Your heart."* A short message with the title "Windows to the Father's Heart" was well-received, and I personally experienced the delight of seeing hope arise in the hearts of the listeners as they realized that Abba was inviting them to "look through windows," so to speak, into His heart in order to discover the many (infinitely many) expressions of His love for us all.

About two weeks after I returned home from that ministry tour in the Pacific Northwest, the Holy Spirit asked me to expand that short message into a day-long workshop and take it on the road. I was delighted, and excited, to do just that. Indeed, there has been such an overwhelming response to the revelations shared during the many subsequent workshops (in both North America and East Africa) that I've been made confident that the time is *now* for writing this encouragement to the body of Christ, and to all those searching for a more intimate relationship with Abba, so that a much larger number of His precious children may be blessed to *"know Him better."*

Windows to the Father's Heart

The format of this book is simple: Each chapter is focused on a particular thematic window, or perspective, into the Father's heart. There is much possible overlap among the various windows; just as when you look from outside through various windows at an object inside a house, you will see (sometimes slightly) different aspects of the same object. It is the same object, but the different perspectives give you an enriched understanding of what that object is like—all its facets. In this case, the "object" is Abba's love for you and me. There is nothing more fascinating in the entire universe.

Grab a fresh cup of your favorite coffee (or tea), and allow Paul's prayer for you to be answered as you gaze through each window. May you rise from your reading with deeper insight into Abba's heart for you and with magnified joy abiding in your soul. I pray that when you realize how much this blesses Abba, in addition to your own rich blessings, *you will be undone by how much you mean to Him.*

My further prayer for you is that you will be absolutely "wrecked beyond recognition" by what you see in your Father's heart, so much so that you will be eager to peer through your own "windows" in order to see more of this infinite, living, dynamic, and overwhelmingly rapturous love-filled heart that is beyond adequate description.

Still further, I pray that the joy that Jesus saw in His future beyond the cross will become yours also, because the treasures you discover in your Father's heart will compel you to share this most glorious love with those who don't yet see what you see. May those who are waiting to hear the good news from you be so captivated by the Father's loving invitation that they will speedily "get out of their chairs."

I believe that your Father is about to answer Paul's prayer (and mine) on your behalf.

Steve Trullinger

The Window of Value

"Father, what is my value in Your sight?"

T his is a question that every believer asks in some form, whether it be expressed directly in prayer or hidden in a capsule of curiosity in the deepest place of yearning in the heart. Perhaps you have received an answer, or several, already as you have pursued this foundational cornerstone of relationship with Abba. He may have spoken to you directly or perhaps through other believers who may have pointed out that the "price" paid by Jesus for you (His sacrificial blood) is a measure of your value. Truly, value measured by the price paid is not a novel diagnostic of worth. In the case of Jesus' blood, it is beyond adequate measure, and hence so is your worth.

But there are other ways as well to gain additional understanding of your value to Abba without diminishing the incredible revelation of the demonstrated measure offered by Jesus through His sacrifice for you. How can we gain additional insight? One of my favorite methods of discovery of Abba's heart attitudes is through their revelation in the nature of His creation in the beginning.

Your Impact in the Beginning

When did you start having an impact on creation? Genesis 1 gives us an answer. As you read the creation account, you will notice that after each stage of creation the writer paused to state something along these

21

lines: "God saw that it was good."[4] Six times in the account[5] we read this self-evaluation of His own work by God before He made Adam and Eve. Not surprising; God doesn't do bad work.

But you may be asking, "Why only six times?" Something must not yet be complete.[6] God was not yet finished; he had yet to create man, as described in Genesis 1:26-29.

Before reading on in Genesis, let's pause to consider how God viewed Adam and his family. A hint is given in the name Adam. This word for "man" is adam. It is used to denote the entire human race, not just the one man.[7] There is a corporate connotation in the word implying the entire race. When Adam (and Eve) appeared on the scene, it is not a stretch to consider that you and I did also. Not only is there the technical residence of us in Adam's body as seed, but perhaps more important for this revelation is God's view of the entire human race through its representative, and progenitor, Adam. When God looked upon Adam, He "saw" you and me and every human being ever to be born. In Abba's heart there was not only Adam but all of us. In other words, he saw us all as a "unit," a family, an "organism" that is not just loosely connected by reproduction. In a very real sense, when Adam and Eve came on the scene, so did you, at least in God's sight.[8]

Now, let's return to the creation account in Genesis 1. Let's focus on verse 31a, after Adam, Eve, and you "appeared on the scene," so to speak:

> God saw **all** that he had made, and it was **very good**
> *(Genesis 1:31a).*

4. In several versions (NIV, NASB, and others) it reads this way or something very similar. In the Amplified Version it reads, "(pleasing, useful) and He affirmed and sustained it"

5. See Genesis 1:4, 10b, 12b, 18b, 21b, 25b.

6. In Hebrew, the number seven indicates completion or fullness.

7. See, for example, the *Tyndale Bible Dictionary* entry entitled, "The Significance of Adam," for more information. Walter A. Elwell and Philip Wesley Comfort, *Tyndale Bible Dictionary* (Carol Stream, IL: Tyndale House Publishers, 2008).

8. This concept of being already "present," or extant, in the body of an ancestor is supported elsewhere in Scripture. For example, note the writer's comment in Hebrews 7:9-10 that Levi could be regarded as having paid "the tenth through Abraham" to Melchizedek, even though he was still in the body of Abraham.

The Window of Value

Note that something is different about this evaluation by God compared to the six previous stage-specific evaluations of the creation components mentioned above—namely, the present use of the adjective *very*. The implication is that, in God's sight, the "goodness" of all of creation prior to man increased, and dramatically so, when Adam (and you) came on the scene.

If you choose to believe this statement, does this mean that you have become arrogant or that your innate arrogance is made manifest? Not necessarily. It is possible to be humble and also believe that you have an immeasurable impact on all of creation at the same time. True humility is exemplified by *agreeing with God*. This is my opinion, but I believe it strongly. If God says we add to the value of the rest of creation, then we do!

Not only is agreement with God a wise decision, it is essential for maintaining humility. In this revelation of your impact on creation, you can agree with God that everything else became better because of you. This is a wise and humble choice.

Think about this deeply, if you dare. God's opinion (as stated in Genesis 1:31a) is that *you* caused all of creation to *go up* on the goodness scale. The stars became better because of *you*. Every tree became better because of you. Every leaf on every tree became better because of you. Even every molecule of air became better because of you. Every grain of sand on every beach became better because of you. The list of possible statements along these lines is endless.

No matter how much you may protest these statements as you attempt to remain "humble," your opinion is most assuredly trumped by God's opinion. It is far better to agree with God, in spite of what you used to believe about yourself, and in so doing gain a glimpse into His heart regarding your value, than to remain falsely humble (a symptom of pride[9]) and claim that you are less valuable than God's assessment. Don't let your lack of understanding of how you could possibly have such an amplifying effect (on all the distant stars, for example) prevent

---

9. False humility is a form of pride because if you claim something different from what God says is the truth concerning you then you have placed your own opinion at a higher level of importance than God's opinion. That is pride.

you from believing God's opinion concerning your impact. He is the Truth, whether we understand His mind or not.

Your Impact after the "Fall" of Adam's Family

After Adam and Eve sinned in the garden (Genesis 3), creation was subjected to frustration and decay,[10] so we can surmise that we (in the bodies of our ancestors) continued to have a profound influence on creation, even in our sinful state. The "goodness" of creation was, sadly, now tarnished or diminished because of the (mysterious) "connection" that we have with the rest of creation.[11] It seems that our influence on creation, as a race called Adam, continued within the framework of God's design in spite of our incomplete understanding of the amplified effect we had outside the sphere of the things we can touch, so to speak.

Your Impact Now: Your "Sonship" Mandate

In case this "action at a distance" on all of creation seems a bit "spooky" or ephemeral, let's take a moment to bring the discussion "down to earth" as we briefly look at your impact on the local environment around you, especially after you joined the family of God through your adoption[12] as a son or daughter of the King. Let me offer just a few examples of your mandate to influence the world around you. As a son of God, you are mandated:

- to set things in right order again[13] (see Genesis 1:26 and 1 John 3:8b);

- to heal the sick, cleanse the leper, raise the dead, and cast out devils (see Matthew 10:8);

- to bring about restoration of all things (see Matthew 17:11);

---

10. See Romans 8:20.

11. Even in a more local and contemporary sense, and from our own limited perspective from a very young age onward, we know that our influence on the world around us was not always good before we were saved. (That's putting it mildly, in my case.)

12. We will also look through The Window of Adoption in this volume.

13. We (Adam) "blew it"; now we have the responsibility and *the opportunity* to "fix it."

- to repair broken walls and restore streets with dwellings (see Isaiah 58:12);

- to proclaim freedom for the captives (see Isaiah 61:1);

- to bind up the brokenhearted (see Isaiah 61:1);

- to proclaim release from darkness for the prisoners (or the blind) (see Isaiah 61:1);

- to be "gushers" of living water (see John 7:38);

- to enlarge Abba's family (see Genesis 1:28a and 9:1; Romans 8:29);

- to usher in the kingdom of heaven upon the earth (see Matthew 6:9-10 and 28:18-20)

- ...and *much* more.

In summary, your mandate is to be like[14] Christ and to do as[15] Christ. Before the foundation of the earth, these good works (and many more) were prepared for you[16] to accomplish.[17] It is probably true that most of us think about the above list (and/or similar examples) when considering our impact, but there is much more coming.

Your Impact in the Future

Returning now to your impact on *all* of creation, the apostle Paul indicates that there is an incredible but yet hidden measure of your value—namely, at the collective "revealing" of the sons of God:

> *For [even the whole] creation [all nature] waits eagerly for the children of God to be revealed* (Romans 8:19 AMP).

Acknowledging that there is a spectrum of opinion concerning when this revelation of the sons of God takes place, our point here is that the

---

14. See Romans 8:29.

15. For example, see John 13:15; 14:12.

16. See Ephesians 2:10. The apostle Paul wrote this letter to the *saints*, or those who have been "reborn" or "recreated" in Christ. See John 3:5-9.

17. But be careful how much value you assign to what you accomplish; the works themselves do not have more value that the worker (*you*).

importance of the sons to *all* of creation is explicit in the New Testament, as well as implied as just studied in the Old Testament.

The strong implication by Paul in Romans 8:19-20 is that the frustration and decay to which the creation was subjected because of the fall of Adam (and you) will be *reversed* by you and the rest of the sons of God. Even though it may not be understood precisely *how* this will happen, nevertheless there will be such a powerful impact on *all* of creation that its "very goodness" will be restored. Not only did you (in Adam) cause creation to become very good in God's sight at the appearance of man, you will again cause this elevation of goodness in the future. This time it will happen because you are in the "second Adam," namely Christ. *Eph 1: 9-10*

Your "sudden" and incredibly enhancing impact on creation happened once, and it will happen again. Meditate on this, and if you have any lingering unworthiness it will be expelled by this revelation concerning your future impact:

> *You will (again) cause **all** of creation to become*
> *"very good."*

I pray that these few insights gained as you look through The Window of Value will whet your appetite for an even deeper revelation of your value in His sight. The fullness of what you will ultimately discover about your value in God's eyes as you explore His heart further is beyond adequate description, let alone prediction. As He shares more of His heart with you in personal ways, you simply will not want to resist His invitation to eternally feast at His table. Your time with Him will grow bigger and deeper. This offer is one that you cannot refuse. His heart is far too amazing and captivating to ignore.

The Window of Adoption

"Father, how did You feel when You adopted me?"

Your identity is encompassed in who your loving Father says you are. That declaration is so rich and textured, so filled with Abba's pride concerning you, and so exquisitely motivated by His heart overflowing with love for you that it seems impossible to fully grasp, at least in a finite amount of time. Even though Abba is the expert in exhibiting clarity embedded in brevity in His communication of facts concerning your identity,[18] He seems to be "unable" to restrain Himself when it comes to expressing His delight[19] in you because of your relationship with Him as His son. For example, His heart overflows as He describes you to the heavenly host.[20] He is so filled with joy because of your adoption as His child that He is seemingly "out of control" with exuberance of heart.

Who Are You?

There are many practical, and even urgent, situations in which it is vitally important to know who you are, or as is often rephrased, *whose* you are. Let's recall the story of the seven sons of Sceva that Luke records in Acts:

---

18. See, for example, his declaration of Gideon's identity in Judges 6:12.

19. See Zephaniah 3:17; the Hebrew word *sûs*, translated as "rejoice" here, can imply ecstatic leaping and twirling in the air. (Strong, *The New Strong's Exhaustive Concordance*, s.v. "sûs," H7797.)

20. You will experience this in the exercise explained in The Window of Pride.

Windows to the Father's Heart

Some Jews who went around driving out evil spirits tried to invoke the name of the Lord Jesus over those who were demon-possessed. They would say, "In the name of Jesus whom Paul preaches, I command you to come out." Seven sons of Sceva, a Jewish chief priest, were doing this. One day the evil spirit answered them, "Jesus I know, and Paul I know about, but who are you?" Then the man who had the evil spirit jumped on them and overpowered them all. He gave them such a beating that they ran out of the house naked and bleeding (Acts 19:13-16).

One obvious inference from this passage is that either the seven sons of Sceva gave no answer to the evil spirit or their answer was not sufficient to cause the spirit to flee. In either case, the spirit was clearly not compelled to submit to their attempt at exorcism, much to their detriment.

I had a personal reminder of the principle in this passage in the spring of 2002 during my first mission to Africa. The setting was a crusade in Tanzania with about 30,000 people on the field who were hungry (or at least curious) to hear what the evangelist was preaching. I was a member of the team of approximately thirty volunteers from North America and served as a "squad" captain to help watch over the welfare of several team members.

Many hundreds of people had already been saved and/or healed earlier on that first night of the five-night crusade, but when the team was sent down to the field in front of the platform to pray for the huge crush of people desperate for healing, the scene became a bit chaotic as our several two-man sub-teams ministered to as many Tanzanians as possible. Although we had each been instructed to stay with our team partner and to not venture far from the platform, the sheer excitement of seeing dozens of people rapidly healed overtook caution as we were literally pulled away from our partners and the platform to pray for more loved ones in the crowd.

The Window of Adoption

That evening at our debriefing, the mission director (mildly) rebuked us for not being obedient to his safety advice. On the next night, everyone was now more alert and obedient as they stayed together with their partners and stuck closer to the platform in case we needed to exit in a hurry.[21] I decided to stay up on the platform and watch over the teams as they ministered to the sick, just in case they might again be drawn too far away from our "safety zone." All was going well on the field in front of the platform as the team members displayed their newfound obedience.

Because all was more "orderly" on the field that second night, I became occupied with rejoicing on the platform as we heard testimony after testimony of healing miracles happening on the field. Suddenly, a team member on the field on the left side of the platform shouted out, "Hey, can somebody give us a hand down here?" I went to investigate and was told by one of our team members that he and his partner had been trying for about fifteen minutes to cast a demon out of the lady who was still writhing like a snake on the grass by the platform. Our two-person team was exhausted and devoid of further strategy.

I asked the Tanzanian ushers nearby to please stand the lady up on her feet in front of me. As they did so, she "calmed" down and seemed to be OK for the moment, standing about three feet in front of me. Just as I was about to command the demon to leave her, she suddenly raised her arm, pointed a finger to my face, and demanded in a man's deep bass, deeper-pitched than was normally possible for a woman,

"Who are you?"

And "she" spoke in English, which we found out later she didn't know. Shades of the seven sons of Sceva. I had several possible options for an answer to this demon. I could have said, for example, "I'm Steve, and I'm on the team," or "Good question, demon. Don't go away, I'll be right back after I check God's Word about who I am," or "I'm Steve;

---

21. Near the end of one of the nights of ministry, our team *did* have to make a hasty exit as a gang of troublemakers with sticks and machetes was spotted marching down a road to the crusade field, presumably to "dissuade" us from preaching about Jesus. Our lookouts spotted them in plenty of time for us to board vans and escape before trouble happened.

I've been anointed by the evangelist," or "I'm Steve; I'm in charge of refreshments." And so on.

I'm making light of the situation, of course, but what actually happened is that when the demon demanded, "Who are you?" I instantly replied, reflexively, without any hesitation whatsoever,

*"I'm a son of God and you're leaving **now**."*

The demon immediately threw the lady back onto the ground, causing her to writhe like a snake a bit more, and then it left her. Praise God. She was free of that demon.[22]

Much more happened during that mission that powerfully impacted me, but that one incident, in which I "answered" the demon with an instant declaration of my sonship, was to prove pivotal over the next few years. Here's why: I was puzzled after that exorcism regarding the immediacy of my "answer." I asked, "Father, how did I know to give that answer, and so quickly at that?" At the moment of confrontation I had no time to ponder possible responses, nor did it occur to me to do so. My answer was so immediate that I was actually shocked by the forceful declaration that came out of my mouth. Here it is again:

*"I'm a son of God, and you're leaving **now**."*

Abba did not delay long in answering my question. He pointed me to a passage in Romans where the apostle Paul encourages the reader regarding their sonship in the kingdom of God:

> *The Spirit you received does not make you slaves, so that you live in fear again; rather, the Spirit you received brought about your adoption to sonship. And by him we cry, "Abba, Father." The Spirit himself testifies with our spirit that we are God's children* (Romans 8:15-16).

---

22. When the lady came up onto the platform to give her testimony, she manifested yet *another* demon and our platform crew cast that one out as well. She later testified to her complete freedom and praised God before the entire crowd.

The Window of Adoption

This was my sought-after answer to the mystery of my super-fast, reflexive reply to the demon. The Spirit of Adoption, namely the Holy Spirit, had in fact *testified* through my own mouth that I was a son of God. This testimony to (and through) my spirit,[23] and to everyone around me at the time, settled any possible lingering doubt on my part that I was a son of the Most High.

Since that encounter in Tanzania in 2002, I have not even once doubted my adoption into the kingdom of God. I went on to study the topic of supernatural adoption in detail and have since given many messages and conducted schools on the subject so that I might somehow encourage my brothers and sisters concerning their identity as sons (and daughters)[24] of God.

Abba's Declaration of Your Sonship

I also learned through my subsequent Bible study on the topic of sonship in the kingdom that Abba is not "bashful" about declaring who His sons are. For example, most believers are familiar I think with the story[25] of Jesus' baptism by His relative[26] John (the Baptist), wherein Abba Himself declares Jesus to be his Son:

> *And a voice from heaven said, "This is my Son, whom I love; with him I am well pleased"* (Matthew 3:17).

> *And a voice came from heaven: "You are my Son, whom I love; with you I am well pleased"* (Mark 1:11; see also Luke 3:22b]

Abba said it again when Jesus was transfigured on a high mountaintop in the presence of Peter, James, and John:

---

23. As a side benefit, I learned firsthand the power of answering from my spirit instead of my soul (mind).

24. The classification, *son of God*, is not gender-exclusive but indicates *relationship* with Abba as His child.

25. See Matthew 3:13-17; Mark 1:9-11; and Luke 3:21, 22.

26. John's mother, Elizabeth, is referred to as a *relative* of Mary, the mother of Jesus. See Luke 1:36.

While he [Peter] was still speaking, a bright cloud covered them, and a voice from the cloud said, "This is my Son, whom I love; with him I am well pleased. Listen to him!" (Matthew 17:5)

Then a cloud appeared and covered them, and a voice came from the cloud: "This is my Son, whom I love. Listen to him!" (Mark 9:7)

A voice came from the cloud, saying, "This is my Son, whom I have chosen; listen to him" (Luke 9:35).

Although these three Gospel writers differ slightly in their phraseology, the clear point is that Abba *declared*, at least twice and in the presence of witnesses, that Jesus was His Son.

It is interesting to note, by the way, that Jesus was not the first to be declared a son of God. Almost 1,000 years before the birth of Jesus, Abba declared to King David (through the prophet Nathan)[27] that he would have a son, to be named Solomon, who would build the house (temple) for God that David himself desired to build (but could not because of how much blood he had shed in his life), and that Solomon would also be God's son. David shared with Solomon what God had told him as he prepared his son for succession to the throne:

But you [David] will have a son who will be a man of peace and rest, and I will give him rest from all his enemies on every side. His name will be Solomon, and I will grant Israel peace and quiet during his reign. He is the one who will build a house for my Name. He will be my son, and I will be his father. And I will establish the throne of his kingdom over Israel forever (1 Chronicles 22:9-10).

David also spoke directly to the officials of Israel, saying:

27. See 2 Samuel 7:13.

The Window of Adoption

Of all my sons—and the Lord has given me many—
he has chosen my son Solomon to sit on the throne of
the kingdom of the Lord over Israel. He said to me:
"Solomon your son is the one who will build my house
and my courts, for I have chosen him to be my son, and I
will be his father" (1 Chronicles 28:5-6).

The above examples are biblical precedents for Abba declaring relationship with His sons. Paul also encourages all believers with the promise that Abba would testify through His Spirit (of Adoption) that we are His sons, both in Romans 8:15-16 and in his letter to the Galatians:

Because you are his sons, God sent the Spirit of his Son
into our hearts, the Spirit who calls out, "Abba, Father."
So you are no longer a slave, but God's child; and
since you are his child, God has made you also an heir
(Galatians 4:6-7).

There is a powerful revelation of identity that occurs because of this infusion of the Holy Spirit (the Spirit of Adoption) into our hearts. Our own voices will join with that of the Spirit of Adoption in declaring that we are sons of God. This is what happened with me on the field in Tanzania when I answered the demon. It will happen (or already has happened) with you if you are a child of God.

The Window of Pride

"Father, how do You brag about me?"

There is a pride that is good. There is a pride that is so good it is beyond measure. It's the pride in Abba's heart because of you.

As we saw when we glimpsed through The Window of Adoption, Abba enjoys making declarations (through different means) of our sonship. There are, in addition, many ways that Abba can (and *does*) make declarations of a related kind concerning His sons and daughters. One of these is through expressions of the *pride* in His heart because of *who you are*.

One day many years ago, as I was in prayer, Abba said this to me: "Son, ask Me the following question." That took me by surprise, so I did what I often do when Father asks me a question in that "out of the blue" manner. I said, "Wait right there, Dad, I will be right back."[28] Then I "whispered" to my Counselor, as I pretended that Abba couldn't hear my surreptitious conversation with my most trusted Advisor, "Holy Spirit, was that Dad asking me to ask Him a question?" He said, "Yes, it's Him. Go ahead; tell Him you are ready to hear the question He wants you to ask of Him."

So I did just that. "Abba, what is the question You want me to ask of You? I am ready to hear it." He answered without any hesitation,

---

28. This is a "game" I often play with Abba, as I pretend He can't hear me asking Holy Spirit for advice. Abba plays along with it and allows me the "fun" of teasing Him.

Windows to the Father's Heart

"Son, ask Me, 'Who do You say I [Steve] am to the heavenly host?'"

I was shocked. First of all, I had no idea that Abba said anything about me to the heavenly host.[29] Second, I wasn't sure I wanted to hear the answer to that question. What if Abba complained to the heavenly host that I was driving Him nuts? What if He was exasperated with me? What if I'd done something so wrong He needed to send an angelic "posse" after me to get me straightened out? What if He was announcing His plans to reserve a place in heaven for me far distant from the throne so He could be spared listening to my bad jokes? What if…?

I'm teasing a bit, of course. But I do believe that many sons of God are tempted to worry about these kinds of things that might be going through the mind of their (supposedly stern) Father. You can rest assured, however, that nothing but good comes out of the Father's mouth concerning you. Even if it is corrective in nature, it is pure in its motivation.[30] He is a loving Father. Nevertheless, it felt a bit risky to invite the Father to tell me the truth, so it took me a few moments to find the courage to ask the question Abba wanted me to pose to Him.

Finally, I was ready. "OK, Dad,

'Who do You say I am to the heavenly host?'"

He had my full attention now. Everything in me was tuned to His voice. I could sense that I was about to be impacted, perhaps forever, by Abba's answer. I waited.

Then He answered the very question He prompted me to ask. I'm not going to share His answer verbatim with you, because it was deeply personal and very intimate and profoundly impacted me. I apologize. Please forgive me. But I will say that it was so good, so encouraging, so uplifting, so life-giving, so full of His "proud Papa" emotion (His own

---

29. By the heavenly host, I knew he meant every being in heaven with ears to hear—all the angels, the four living creatures, the twenty-four elders, the great cloud of witnesses, and so on.

30. See Hebrews 12:5-11; see also Matthew 4:4.

"joy inexpressible and full of glory"[31]) in adopting me as His son that I was reduced to a "bawling pile of mush" for a good half hour with half a box of used tissues to bear witness.

Abba Brags about You

Based on my own experience and that of many other sons of God, as well as what is written in the Scriptures, I want to declare to you that:

*Abba **brags** about you to the heavenly host.*

I hope I can help you believe this statement. Let me first remind you of what the Lord said concerning Job:

> *One day the angels came to present themselves before the Lord, and Satan also came with them. The Lord said to Satan, "Where have you come from?" Satan answered the Lord, "From roaming throughout the earth, going back and forth on it." Then the Lord said to Satan, "Have you considered my servant Job? There is no one on earth like him; he is blameless and upright, a man who fears God and shuns evil"* (Job 1:6-8; see also Job 2:1-3).

The Lord was *bragging* about Job. Not only did Satan hear God bragging about His son, it is likely that all the angels heard Him as well because they were also assembled before the Lord. The Lord bragged *again* about Job in chapter 2:1-3. So, He bragged not just once but *twice*.

Next, we need to remember that God does not show partiality (Proverbs 28:21) or favoritism (Acts 10:34; Ephesians 6:9). It may help to also remember that Jesus Himself declared that you (as a believer) are greater than Job, because John the Baptist was greater than everyone born of women up to that time, and you are greater than John:

> *Truly I tell you, among those born of women there has not risen anyone greater than John the Baptist; yet*

---

31. See 1 Peter 1:8.

Windows to the Father's Heart

whoever is least in the kingdom of heaven is greater than he (Matthew 11:11).

We are motivated to claim the following:

God bragged about Job, and He brags about **you**.

Let's explore how Abba feels about you as a son (or daughter) with an illustration. The setting is a Little League baseball game. There are two dugouts that house the teams when they are alternately "at bat"— one along the first-base line and the other along the third-base line of the baseball diamond. Somewhere close behind the dugouts are sets of bleachers where the parents and friends of the players take their cheerleader positions to encourage their respective teams.

Imagine that Johnny is playing center field as an outfielder during the first half of the last inning, and their team is behind by three runs. Johnny makes a spectacular diving catch for a fly ball, one that seemed impossible to snag, for the third and final "out" in a crucial play. His action saves the inning from additional dreaded scores by the opposing team. With the bleachers of cheerleaders (mostly parents) for Johnny's team erupting in applause and shouting at the top of their lungs, his team triumphantly runs to their dugout near the "screamers" and proceeds to high-five each other with mutual congratulations. The boys can hardly contain themselves as they try to settle down and prepare for their turn at bat. They need four runs to win.

Johnny's dad is in the bleachers behind his son's dugout. He waits patiently for the noise in the dugout to die down a bit. Then he declares to the other parents next to him in the bleachers, and just loudly enough for Johnny to hear, "Did you guys see that play Johnny made? Wasn't he amazing?" Johnny's ears perk up as he catches the voice of his dad in the bleachers, bragging about him. Beaming from ear to ear, Johnny lets his dad's praise soak deep down in his soul as the revelation cements in his mind: "My dad is so proud of me. Wow!" With newly heightened confidence, Johnny eventually gets his turn at bat. The bases are loaded and he hits a home run to score the four runs and win the game. Go, Johnny! (It's appropriate to cheer at this point.)

Johnny's dad was purposeful in praising his son, not only in front of the parents of the other boys on Johnny's team, but especially loud enough for Johnny to hear in the dugout. If Johnny's dad was purposeful in his bragging about his son in a baseball game, how much more does your Abba desire to encourage you by declaring loudly to the whole heavenly host how wonderful you are? I hope you will agree with the following statement and, even more, receive it deep in your soul as a life-changing truth that will set you free[32] from self-condemnation, unworthiness, and all that goes with them.

> *Your Abba brags about **you** in heaven loudly enough for*
> ***you** to hear.*

Again, your Abba doesn't just brag about you in secret to the heavenly host; He wants *you* to hear Him doing it. He loves you so much that He wants you to *know* how proud He is of you.

Exercise: Respond to Abba's Invitation to "Eavesdrop"

Your Abba wants you to hear just how proud He is of you. He invites you to "eavesdrop" as he brags, just as He did for me several years ago. I encourage you to take a few moments, get quiet before the Lord, and ask Abba this question:

> *"Daddy, what do You say about me to the heavenly*
> *host?"*

Be sure to write down His answer(s). Try not to filter out something that seems "too good to be true"—write it down anyway.[33] Try to capture the impressions you get as you listen. They may come as actual words, visions, Scripture, songs, or feelings of deep value and worth. Abba is

---

32. See John 8:31-32.

33. But *do* filter out anything you hear that *isn't* amazing, edifying, or encouraging. If what you are hearing doesn't build up and make you feel good, it's not from Abba.

able to communicate in ways that work for *you*. Be sure to have a box of tissues handy.

Group Exercise: Eavesdropping for One Another

Next, try a variation of this exercise when you have some time with a prayer group or during a Bible study, fellowship meeting, or home church. With the approval and support of your group leader, have everyone go through the first exercise of individual eavesdropping on Abba's bragging, writing down what they hear and sense. Then ask everyone to choose a partner[34] for this next exercise, preferably someone who doesn't know them as well as their long-time friend, spouse, or significant other.

In each partnership of two people, the first partner will assume the role of eavesdropper on behalf of their partner. In other words, they will "listen in" or directly ask Abba to tell them what He says about their partner to the heavenly host. At the same time, the second partner should pray silently, asking Abba, "Yes, Daddy, tell my partner what You say about me to the heavenly host." In this scenario, there are two saints agreeing in prayer[35] about something that Abba *wants to do already*. The first partner should write down what they "hear" regarding Abba's bragging about the second partner.[36]

After the partners are finished[37] with writing down what Abba says about their partner, then the partners should switch roles, allowing the second partner to write what Abba brags about the first partner as the first partner implores Abba to help the second partner "listen in."

---

34. If there is an odd number of people in the group, then form a threesome for this part of the exercise so that no one is left out.

35. See Matthew 18:19.

36. For a threesome, have *two* partners simultaneously eavesdrop on behalf of the third partner, while the third partner prays, "Yes, Daddy, tell my two partners what You say about me to the heavenly host." Then switch roles twice until this has been done on behalf of each partner.

37. If some partners need more time to finish listening to what God is speaking, encourage them to do so at a break time or perhaps after the meeting or another time suitable for both.

The Window of Pride

Once everyone is finished (within a reasonable time), then the fun begins as the partners share with each other what they heard on behalf of each other. As I have conducted this exercise with numerous groups of saints over the years, I almost always have had difficulty regaining "control" of the session. This is because the excitement level crescendos as most of the people hear confirmations through their partner of what Abba was sharing with them directly. Even if their partner has heard something different, it is always good[38] and simply reflects additional bragging that Abba is doing. It is wise to have boxes of tissues handy when you do this exercise. ☺

This exercise can be repeated with other partners as often as desired and as time allows. I have yet to find anyone who objected to hearing how much Abba brags about them to the entire heavenly host. This desire and the delight we find in it is akin to that of a child asking to hear the same favorite bedtime story every night before falling asleep. I personally repeat this exercise often. Whenever I do it I am wrecked[39] with Abba's delight in me. And because I am so powerfully impacted by my Abba's pride in me, He is wrecked more than I am.[40]

Let me share this last statement as a general principle, one that will appear (perhaps in different forms) in several of our "window glimpses:"

*When **you** are blessed, your Abba is blessed.*

Let the reality of the effect that you have on Abba's heart sink into your soul. We will revisit it often.

---

38. If your partner hasn't heard something "good" in Abba's bragging about you, then choose a different partner. ☺

39. A not-so-theological term for "blessed beyond measure."

40. The concept of the divine escalation of blessing will be discussed further as we look through The Window of Joy.

The Window of Pleasure

"Father, how do I give You pleasure?"

At some point in our maturation as sons of God, it becomes a priority for us to find ways to please our Father in heaven. Hopefully this is not because we want to try to "earn" more favor or acceptance from Him, but simply because we love Him and want His heart to be gladdened because of us. Every healthy, vibrant relationship we have always provides for two-way paths of blessing so that the person we care about isn't the only one giving unconditionally. Our relationship with Abba as His son or daughter is no exception.

In the nurturing relationship you have with Abba, it is surely important (to you and to Him) that you search His heart to find out what pleases Him about you in particular. Deep down in your soul, you want to know how you can please your Father because you love Him with childlike[41] adoration. Even if you haven't been blessed with this kind of desire or opportunity in your relationship with your earthly father, you now have it with Abba because you've been reborn into the most glorious, tender, and safe[42] parental care in the universe.

Pleasure before Performance

It is good to remember that Abba's pleasure with you began before you had anything to do with it directly.

41. See Mark 10:15 and Luke 18:17.
42. See, for example, Psalm 91.

43

Windows to the Father's Heart

He predestined us for adoption to sonship through Jesus Christ, in accordance with his pleasure and will (Ephesians 1:5).

Daddy couldn't wait for you to "show up" before He started experiencing pleasure because of you. In a similar vein, Daddy didn't wait until you started doing stuff for His kingdom (e.g., miracles, signs, wonders, or good works[43] in general) in order to have pleasure in you. This we know because of the example of Jesus bringing His Father pleasure before his official ministry began at the age of thirty.

*And a voice came from heaven: "You are my Son, whom I love; with you I am well **pleased**"* (Mark 1:11; see also Luke 3:22b).

Abba loves you in the same manner and degree that He loves Jesus[44]; you may be sure that He was pleased with you *before* your "ministry" began. This bears repeating:

*Abba was pleased with you **before** you did anything for Him.*

In addition, Abba derived pleasure through another, seemingly one-sided action on His part:

Now if we are children, then we are heirs—heirs of God and co-heirs with Christ (Romans 8:17a).

Your Father has been pleased to give you the kingdom (Luke 12:32).

Note the past tense used in Luke 12:32. You've been given the kingdom as an heir of God. That was Abba's decision, not yours. He decided to give you this gift *before* you could even think to ask for it. And it *pleased* Him to do so.

---

43. See Ephesians 2:10.

44. See John 17:23, 26.

The Window of Pleasure

This unearned pleasure that God has with us is an attribute of His heart. It defies complete understanding. This mystery fills (and thrills) our own hearts. Most parents can attest that they experience delight in the very existence of each of their children. This delight has nothing at all to do with that child's performance. In fact, it precedes the child's ability to perform. This is the best illustration we have of this preemptory blessing that Abba experiences over each of us.

Pleasure in Our Choices

Abba does, however, take pleasure because of some of our actions. There are many examples, but I want to focus on one particular type of pleasure we can bring Abba that is based on our active involvement in His heart—our choices[45] that are based on an aspect of His character, like His *faithfulness*.

Years ago I discovered something as I was preparing a message on building faith. I realized that I didn't really understand the biblical difference between *faith* and *belief*. It seemed to me that Jesus used those terms almost interchangeably.[46] I invested a considerable amount of time in searching the Scriptures for clues and arrived at one possible way to view them. It can be summarized succinctly this way:

*Faith is a **gift**; belief is a **choice**.*

Faith can be viewed as an *enablement*[47] from God to make choices to believe. The difference is sometimes subtle and is discussed at more length in the message that I did eventually prepare on building belief.[48]

---

45. We will look at the broader context of choice-making in The Window of Choice.

46. Interestingly, I later learned that in some languages, like Korean, there are not two separate words for the English terms *faith* and *belief*.

47. See, for examples, Ephesians 2:8-9 and Romans 12:3.

48. See "Unmasking Unbelief," which may still be available for download as a two-part mp3 audio message using these links: https://db.tt/sIv6f0nB and https://db.tt/v4QVXQRW

Windows to the Father's Heart

As we pursue the question of how our choices to believe can please Abba, it is important to distinguish between the gift (faith) and what we do with it (choice). The following excerpt from Hebrews 11:6 is often memorized by believers and relied upon to emphasize the importance of faith:

> *And without faith it is impossible to please God*
> (Hebrews 11:6).

Please note that this verse does not state that "faith pleases God" but rather it states that we must have it in order to please God. In other words, faith is a necessary but not sufficient condition for pleasing God. We need to be careful not to read more into the verse than it actually states.

Let me illustrate the point of these remarks with a simple scenario. Suppose a loving father gives his eight-year-old daughter a brand-new bicycle for her birthday. Is it the bicycle (the gift) that pleases the father or what his daughter does with it (rides it)? Of course the answer is the latter. If his daughter leaves the bicycle in the garage for six months and never touches it, the father will surely be disappointed.

In like manner, the gift is not what pleases the Giver (Abba); it is what His child (you) does with it that pleases Him. When you make a choice to believe God using the faith He has given you, what you are essentially doing is giving expression to your faith by demonstrating that you really do trust God's faithfulness to deliver on His promises.[49] Unbelief, on the other hand, is also a choice—namely, to disbelieve God and not trust His faithfulness.

There are families of unbelief; these are areas in which unbelief manifests itself in a believer. One of them has to do with the numerous types of fear that can beset someone. Another includes refusal to believe the statements God has made concerning our value, worth, and abilities. In the table below, I've listed a few representatives of some similar categories. In each example you will find the area of unbelief and some sample Scriptures that have been ignored/disobeyed in making the choice

---

49. See 2 Corinthians 1:20.

to do that. Though this list is far from complete, you may see clearly that unbelief is a choice rather than something that "just happens to you."

Unbelief as a Choice

Manifestation/ "mask" of unbelief	Choice to not believe that God...	Sample Scriptures of promise / declaration
Fear of harm	...will protect you.	Psalm 91
Fear of lack	...will provide for you.	Matthew 6:25-33; Luke 12:22-31
Fear of abandonment	...will always be with you.	Deuteronomy 31:8; Joshua 1:5; Psalms 37:28; 94:14; Isaiah 42:16; Matthew 28:20; Hebrews 13:5
Fear of failure / lack of confidence	...will strongly support you.	2 Chronicles 16:9; Judges 6:15-16; Mark 9:23; Philippians 4:13 (AMP)
"Can't be done."	...can do anything with you.	Mark 9:23
Persistent guilt/shame	...has forgiven you.	Psalms 103:12; Isaiah 43:25; Hebrews 8:12; 10:17; 1 John 2:12
Unworthiness	...has declared your worth.	Matthew 6:26
Self-condemnation	...has removed condemnation.	Romans 8:1
Bondage to the past ("If only things could be the way they were...")	...has planned your good future.	Jeremiah 29:11
Bondage to the future ("I'll be all set when...")	...has already given you the kingdom.	Luke 12:32

The good news is that when you do make a choice to believe Abba's promise or declaration (for examples, see Column 2 in the table above), then His heart is blessed. He experiences pleasure because of your choice. The foundational reason for His pleasure is that your choice to believe Him leads to blessings in your life or circumstances, and your blessing causes Him to be blessed, which in turn brings you more blessing.[50] Let me summarize with this principle:

*Abba is **pleased** when you choose to believe Him.*

This feature of the Father's heart is evident in many different ways, but they are all rooted in His amazing love for you.

Choose today to "warm" your Abba's heart by believing His promises and His declarations that you have previously disbelieved. When you are focused on His love for you, this repentance becomes much less onerous or, put another way, it isn't such a tough pill to swallow. True freedom is fostered in an atmosphere of trust in Abba's faithfulness, and your freedom greatly pleases Him.

There are many other ways that we bring pleasure to Abba, of course, and we will explore some of these in The Window of Joy, and others will take the forefront as we look through several of the additional windows included in this volume. But one in particular merits some highlighting here—namely, the pleasure Abba has in regarding you as an extension of Himself. This is not to say that He "needed" more of Himself because He was somehow incomplete or insufficient, but rather that His perfect will contained the best possible expression of His love—*you*. It is a mystery that Abba requires *your* existence as part of His completeness.

Abba's Image, Our Pleasure

Have you ever wondered why God made you in *His* image and not completely different?[51] This is a very deep question in itself, and our understanding of His motivation is necessarily incomplete because His

---

50. This is what I call "divine escalation of blessing."

51. Of course, God the Father is Spirit and we have bodily form, but here "image" refers to likeness, similar attributes, resemblance, and being a reflection of His character through our inherent nature.

thoughts are *higher* than our thoughts.[52] However, let's focus on His pleasure in making you in *His* image. This gives us wonderful insight into His heart of love for His children.

In making you in His image, Abba was not practicing self-idolatry. He wasn't practicing self-*anything*. He had in mind *your* pleasure in being like *Him*. This bears repeating:

*Abba foresaw **your** pleasure in being like **Him**.*

We will explore this further in other chapters, but here we take note of Abba's love for us manifesting through His desire to bless us with His goodness, the glory of His nature. Being aware of His own perfection and desiring the very best for us in designing our nature, Abba did not display arrogance in making us like Him, but rather His own agreement with the Truth, His Son.

Put another way, Abba desired (and desires) the very best for us, and whose image would be better than His? Here again, we see Abba's "others-focused" nature that *must* be congruent with His nature that can only practice perfect love. There is no room for self-focus in God. He is love and by that very nature He cannot be "about Himself" in His focus, attitudes, and behavior. From the beginning, He predestined us to be conformed to the image of His Son[53] so that we might inherit *every* spiritual blessing in Christ.[54]

This sharing nature of Abba's heart is evident throughout His creation, but perhaps most clearly through His perfect reflection— Jesus.[55] In becoming one with Jesus,[56] we experience the fullness of God's divine nature[57] including partaking[58] in His pleasure. He

52. See Isaiah 55:9.

53. See Romans 8:29.

54. See Ephesians 1:3.

55. See Hebrews 1:3.

56. For example, see John 17:20-23.

57. See Colossians 2:9-10.

58. See 2 Peter 1:4.

shares His very *life* with you,[59] which includes the full measure of His joy.[60] Put another way,

> *Abba takes pleasure in **your** pleasure.*

He is such a good Dad.

---

59. See Galatians 2:20.
60. See John 15:11 and 17:13.

The Window of Choice

"Father, why did You give me free will?"

Although we have already looked at how we can give Abba pleasure with our choice(s) to believe Him, there is a much broader perspective that helps us see even more of the love in His heart. He is a decision-maker, and you are made in His image. That fact alone might be sufficient to explain why you have free will, but let's probe more deeply into Abba's heart through The Window of Choice.

Priorities Motivate Choices

Let me share a story from my boyhood, a profound experience that shaped my life for the decades to come afterward. My relationship with my earthly father during my boyhood was great. I thoroughly enjoyed the times I had with my dad growing up in the beautiful Pacific Northwest. Although I was born in Eugene, Oregon and have fond memories from my early childhood, most of my memories involving Dad occurred after we moved to Portland when I was eight years old.

As a "young man to be," I relished all the ways my dad shaped me. He was a gifted musician and taught me how to play the piano; he taught me how to use tools and how to build what I might need (in the way of forts, clubhouses, chemistry labs, science projects, and so on). He taught me sports and we spent countless hours playing catch with a baseball[61] and attending several minor league games at Multnomah

---

61. Our boys' baseball team placed second in the state, and we only lost the championship

51

Stadium in Portland. He taught me about business, and I had two profitable businesses by the age of twelve. We were active together in the Boy Scouts and went camping often (Dad was the leader of the District Council for the Boy Scouts in the Portland area). He taught me about community involvement and activism for the good of the city and showed me, by example, the importance of developing solid relationships in our neighborhood. My dad was well respected as a leader in every arena in which he participated.

As you may have guessed by now, my dad was my hero. I wanted so much to be like him "when I grew up" that I could taste it. But my purpose in sharing these things is not so much to brag about Dad. I want to be sensitive to those readers who may not have had such a great relationship with their earthly fathers. My purpose in sharing all this is to give you a bit of the backstory before the storm. When I was thirteen years old, right in the prime of enjoying my relationship with Dad, my world fell apart when my parents divorced. My dad remarried quickly in a neighboring state and inherited two stepsons and a stepdaughter in the process. I missed my dad beyond measure. That year was extremely painful. I did not realize at the time just how much pain filled my heart, but it became crystal clear when my dad got a promotion at work and transferred to the Los Angeles area.

On the day of his move in August 1964, he stopped through town to pick up some belongings and say goodbye to his kids before driving south to Los Angeles. I was brokenhearted when my dad came in the house for his farewell hugs, leaving his station wagon in the driveway loaded with his new family and with a small trailer hitched behind to carry luggage and a few small belongings. All I could say through my tears was,

"Dad, I want to go with you."

I was distraught, and my parents asked me why I wanted to go. It was a reasonable question. They needed to make sure it wasn't some

---

game by one run in three extra innings, but that's another story.

kind of momentary desire on my part. I was so upset, however, that I couldn't even talk through my sobs. They asked me to go to my room and write out the reasons I wanted to go. I did, but I don't remember what I listed on the paper. Whatever I wrote, it worked, because Mom agreed to let me go with Dad. She could see just how important it was for me to be with Dad, and her mother's love compelled her to sacrifice a part of her heart to release me.

Mom helped me pack a suitcase quickly and I threw it into the trailer behind my dad's station wagon, hopped into the car with my new family (who may or may not have been waiting patiently), and headed off to California. I don't remember even having time to say goodbye to my brother, my sister, my live-in grandmother, or any of my friends. That was it. A sudden shift in my life that was quite dramatic and costly.

Nothing else mattered to me, however, as much as being with Dad. I truly did not consider the sacrifices I was making in relationships by moving to California. Those were not even on my radar. Being with Dad was my consuming focus. My priority motivated my choice.

Desperate for Dad

My reason for sharing this is twofold. First, my hope is that you will have some insight into my personal quest for discovering the heart of my Abba based on the depth of my relationship with my earthly father. Second, this experience gave me a grid for desiring to always be desperate for my heavenly Father. I always want Him to be the focus of my heart, and strongly so.

Jesus admonished us to have this kind of single-mindedness in our priorities concerning relationships:

> *If anyone comes to me and does not hate father and mother, wife and children, brothers and sisters—yes, even their own life—such a person cannot be my disciple* (Luke 14:26).

Jesus has challenged us to make *God* the utmost priority in our lives, so much so that our love for our family members should "look like hatred" in comparison to our love for Him. Jesus is not advocating hatred but making a strong point about the required preeminence God should have in our priority system. If our priorities are lined up the way Jesus taught, then we will not hesitate when making difficult choices.

Passion Motivates Curiosity

You may recall my salvation story in the Introduction. My revelation of my Father's love ignited a curiosity to know His heart; hence, my frequent prayer:

"Daddy, show me more of Your heart."

My passion to somehow "capture" more of this amazing love coming from Abba birthed my desire to understand his "Father-heart." And my passion to understand my sonship in the kingdom motivated (and still motivates) my curiosity to understand fatherhood. Because I'm seeking to understand a relationship, I must be prepared to explore the hearts of both father and son.

This theme of the interconnectedness of the hearts of Father and Son pervades our window glimpses. As any serious student of relationships soon learns, it is not possible to fully understand a good relationship by simply examining how well each person satisfies the other's needs. A deep understanding of a successful, loving relationship requires the discovery of how well each person values the needs of the *other* above their own.

In other words, to truly appreciate their passionate love for one another we must recognize and appreciate the shift that has taken place in their lives—from self-focus to an others-focus. A heart that is passionate for another person is evidenced by unquenchable curiosity concerning and concomitant discovery of the feelings resident in the other's heart. One cannot be passionate for another person without being irresistibly curious about what kind of emotional treasure can be found in their "ticker."

You may have heard the old expression, "Curiosity killed the cat." Curiosity regarding the Father's heart is not quite that dangerous, but it does carry a "warning label" because the process of learning about Abba's heart is not just observational but very often is (perhaps unexpectedly) participatory. For example, when you probe Abba's heart to learn about unconditional love, He does not show you a documentary on the life of Jesus (as amazing as that would be). Instead, you may find that a person suddenly appears in your life who is very difficult to love and they seem to have little chance of loving you back. As you grow in your ability to love this person unconditionally, you gain a deeper appreciation of how much Abba loves you without condition.

Your Place in Abba's Heart

Many years ago I had a vision that relates directly to the gift of free will God has given us. The setting was a small conference at a wonderful community church in Pasadena, California, and I was standing in the front row during a time of corporate worship of the Lord with music and songs from the heart. As I was experiencing the sweet presence of the Lord, I was riveted by a vision, seen with my eyes open, of a portion of Abba's heart. It was not shaped like a valentine, but I knew by the Spirit that I was getting a glimpse of my Father's heart, alive and full of love.

As I stared at Abba's heart, I saw a gingerbread man-shaped hole in it. It had a head, two arms and two legs. I asked Abba what that hole was in His heart, and he answered, "Son, that hole in My heart has your shape." I joked a bit, saying that it looked skinnier than I was. (Yes, you can joke with Abba—He has a great sense of humor.[62]) I asked, "Are You nudging me to lose weight, Abba?"

---

62. Abba's sense of humor is a lot like mine—and *yours*. We will explore more of it when we look through The Window of Fun in a future volume.

Windows to the Father's Heart

Before He could tease me about that, the scene changed and now I was seeing a much larger portion of His heart, extending as far as I could see both to my left and to my right. Instead of just one man-shaped hole in His heart, there was now an enormous chain of man-shaped holes, side by side and connected fingertip to fingertip, extending as far as I could see in both directions. The chain resembled a gigantic version of a child's string of paper-doll cutouts. I was mystified by what I was seeing. I asked, "What are all these holes in Your heart, Father?" He answered right away, "Son, there is a hole in My heart for every one of My children."

There is a hole in your Father's heart with your shape.

I began to weep as I realized that some of those holes in Abba's heart would never be filled. I began to feel at least an infinitesimal bit of the pain that Abba endures when even one of His children refuses to take their place in His heart, let alone the billions who have refused the special places individually crafted for them. The pain was indescribable and nearly incapacitated me, so much so that the conference organizer asked if I was OK. I managed to describe a little of what I was seeing, and a few moments later was asked to share it with the rest of the conference attendees, many of whom also began to weep.

I want to pursue further the implications of these empty holes in the Father's heart, but first I should relate the next scene in the vision. I saw someone trying to force their way into a hole in Abba's heart that was not for them but for someone else. I was reminded of a young child playing with a pegboard, trying to hammer a square-shaped peg into a round hole. I could hear the Father yelping in pain as this person tried to forcibly occupy a place in the Father's heart that was not intended for them. Then I saw a hand gently take the person by their hand, guiding them to their place. I heard Abba's voice gently and lovingly saying to them, "Here is your place in My heart; you will fit perfectly here."

Not only was the lesson made clear that we should not try to be like anyone else—because if we do it causes Abba pain in His heart—

but this part of the vision also drove home the lesson that Abba has meticulously crafted a place in His heart for each of us and only we can fill that place. No one else can. This is just one way Abba demonstrates His immeasurable attention to every aspect of our lives and being.

> *No one else can fill the hole in Abba's heart reserved*
> *for **you** alone.*

In other words, if *you* don't fill your place in Abba's heart by accepting His offer of sonship (adoption) through belief in His Son Jesus, then *no one else can.*

This brings me to a profound revelation concerning the Father's love. The refusal by some of His children to occupy the places reserved for them in His heart means that those special, individual places will remain empty *forever*. This, in turn, implies that Father has, and will eternally have, pain in His heart because of the rebellion of children who never come home. This is the pain that I "tasted" ever so slightly during my vision. It was unbearable to me, and yet I know I felt only a tiny fraction of the pain Abba experiences and will experience forever.

> *Unfilled holes in Abba's heart hurt Him forever.*

For some reason, He has chosen to make Himself vulnerable to the possibility of this eternal pain. *Why*?

Abba's Risk

The question of whether Abba risks anything at all, because of His omniscience,[63] is a deep question beyond the capacity of this author to answer to the satisfaction of all theologians, let alone everyone else in the body of Christ. But I will hazard sharing my opinion, because it is based not only on God's Word but also on decades of discovery of God's heart as He chose to reveal it to me. To be sure, my understanding is incomplete, and necessarily so:

---

63. The intriguing question of whether God sometimes limits His own knowledge can, and likely *will*, keep theologians busy for a long, long time. The interested reader may wish to sink his or her teeth into the general subject of *open theism* for more insights.

Windows to the Father's Heart

"For my thoughts are not your thoughts, neither are your ways my ways," declares the Lord. "As the heavens are higher than the earth, so are my ways higher than your ways and my thoughts than your thoughts" (Isaiah 55:8-9).

I want to be clear about my speculations (of which there are many in this book[64]) as opposed to declarations of doctrine. I also want to encourage you to imitate the Bereans, who were declared to be nobler than the Thessalonians in Acts 17:11 because they searched the Word of God to ascertain the truth of the teaching and preaching they heard. Check the Scriptures for yourself to see if what I'm writing is true.

My claim that Abba chooses to risk possibly eternal pain (because of our possible rebellious rejection of His offer of adoption as a son) is motivated by a realization of His overarching love for us as demonstrated by His gift of free will. Out of His great love, He intentionally chose to risk the eternal pain of your refusal of sonship so that He might give you the incredible gift of free will and gain you through your own choice. He gave up His control to give us a choice. Said still another way,

Abba's love-gift of free will trumps His risk of eternal pain of rejection by you.

Abba's pain if you reject Him is not because of a focus on Himself. Instead, it is the pain of enduring *your* pain. At the end of my vision, Abba concluded with another truth about my heart: "Son, in addition to a hole in My heart with your shape, there is a hole in *your* heart with *My* shape, and only *I* can fill it." If you reject Abba's invitation to adoption in His family, then there are *two* holes left unfilled for eternity. Pain produced by such eternal separation is felt in both hearts; that is the nature of intimate relationship.

---

64. See, for example, the chapter entitled The Window of Curiosity for some related questions. Here is just *one* question to ponder: "As we are made in God's image, how could He have given us *curiosity* if He himself did not have it?"

The Window of Choice

On a positive note, the price Abba paid in making His heart vulnerable to rejection by His children, by giving them the amazing gift of free will, has given us tremendous insight into His limitless love, a love that expresses itself in literally countless ways. Because we have free will, we have the potentiality of boundless joy as we make (good) choices. Abba knows this potentiality, having *invented* it, and delights in our wise exercise of this gift.

The Window of the Future

"Father, how do You feel about my future?"

It is surely an understatement to say that Abba is ridiculously excited about your future. There are no words sufficient to describe how He feels about the future that awaits you. This is such a vast window into the Father's heart that it overlaps with The Window of Eternity, The Window of Trust, The Window of Support, and others.

How Important to the Father Are His Plans for You?

> *"For I know the plans I have for you," declares the Lord,*
> *"plans to prosper you and not to harm you, plans to give*
> *you hope and a future"* (Jeremiah 29:11).

This verse can arguably be regarded as one of the all-time favorite verses among Christians all over the world. I've seen it painted on the interior walls of churches; it is on church website banners; it graces the letterhead of many pastors; and it can be found on Bible covers, bookmarks, coffee mugs, and much more. It is memorized by many believers early[65] in their program of study of the Bible.

Why is this verse so popular? The answer is very obvious. It is one of the most encouraging verses in all of Scripture, without any negative aspect whatsoever. It is a clear declaration of Abba's intense desire for you and me to have belief in His goodness toward us. It was delivered through Jeremiah to the exiles in the Babylonian captivity as a life-

---

65. Jeremiah 29:11 is the very first verse that I committed to memory as a new Christian.

giving message of hope and a reminder that God intended to fulfill His promise to bring the exiles back to the land of Israel. Today, this verse still brings powerful hope and encouragement to all who call upon His name because it illustrates Abba's loving kindness toward all of His children.

But there is more. Jeremiah 29:11 contains more than encouragement, more than an uplifting of our hearts, more than hope for the future. It contains a declaration of Abba's very nature and of your importance, and the importance of your future, to Him. Let me explain. The Hebrew word translated as "know" in Jeremiah 29:11 is yada.[66] It means much more than just awareness. It implies full, complete, intimate, relational knowledge of the kind shared by husband and wife. Indeed, it implies the involvement of the whole being, not just the mind but including the will and emotions as well.[67]

In the Hebrew way of thinking, the thoughts (plans) of a man are not separate from the man, as opposed to the Hellenistic (Greek) view of thoughts as being superior to the thinker. The Hebrew reader of Jeremiah would already understand that God's thoughts (plans) are not separate from God. They are an integral part of Him. In other words, He could no more separate Himself from His plans for you than He could separate Himself from the Holy Spirit.

When we consider the love expression of Abba in Jeremiah 29:11, we can see His declaration that He regards His plans for us as treasures that He cherishes in His heart. They are not occasional remembrances that flit through His mind once in a while. No! He constantly meditates on His plans for you. They are not kept on the back burner or stuffed on some dusty shelf in the library of heaven. He never stops rejoicing in His plans for you. Let me summarize how important your future is to Abba:

*Your future is a **part** of God.*

We have been trained to dissect our thoughts and those of others as though they were separate from the one who thought them, so this concept may be hard to grasp. As you increasingly incorporate this reality into

---

66. Strong, *The New Strong's Exhaustive Concordance*, s.v. "yada," H3045.

67. See, for example, the entry for "knowledge" in *Tyndale's Bible Dictionary*.

your own view of Abba's heart, you will experience a growing intimacy with Him. This true relationship will eventually overpower the more analytical, clinical, and even sterile view of God's thoughts toward His children that has for so long inhibited relationship with Him. It is vital for us to grow to love Abba's thoughts because they are a portion of Him; they are part of His very nature or essence. It is also vital that we come to realize that He is our portion and we are never separate from Him. We are one.

Abba's Thoughts Are Lovable

There is tremendous blessing in embracing this dimension of what it means to love Abba. If you learn to increase your passionate love of Abba's thoughts,[68] you will increasingly love His thoughts toward your brothers and sisters in Christ and not just His thoughts toward you. Your love for others will grow in new dimensions of expression and in its impact on those around you. Your focus on others will increase while your focus on yourself will decrease. Your love for others will become more like Christ's love for them as you share in Abba's thoughts toward them.

Prophecy

From this perspective, though it may be a bit unfamiliar, the love of Abba's thoughts toward others is a huge part of what it means to be one[69] with your Father. In order to more fully see into your Father's heart and understand more of His loving nature, the quest for this love of His thoughts toward others necessarily entails the experience of adopting His value for your brethren and His compassion for them. Jesus modeled this beautifully for us throughout His life and ministry on earth and via His living expression of love through His disciples.

Abba Loves Your Plans

There is an ignition of joy in the heart of your Abba when He considers your plans for the future. Many believers, however, often joke as they consider God "laughing" at their plans (or someone else's

---

68. See David's view in Psalms 139:17-18.

69. See John 17:20-23.

plans) because they think He is laughing in derision at the silliness or immaturity of those plans. That may be true regarding plans that are selfishly motivated, intent on harm, or have some other component of wickedness in them, but when your plans are infused with love and touch His heart because of their Christlikeness, then Abba rejoices beyond measure.

Think about how a parent feels when their child announces his or her intent to conquer the world or some part of it. Rather than responding with derision at such an announcement, the child's plans are regarded as cute; they bring a smile to the parent's face. Joy wells up in the parent's heart as they realize that the independent thoughts of their child are an expression of the free will they have been given and evidence the personhood of their child. The parent feels joy for many reasons at such times, but one of those comes from the realization that their child is a "little me."

The Father's joy springing from your plans is similar but immeasurable. There is a place in His heart that regards your thoughts as precious. Your Christlike thoughts and plans are considered by Abba as "extensions," in a sense, of His own being. This "oneness" with God is an aspect of your sonship in His family. Remember that Abba regards Adam's family[70] as a unit—an organism, if you will. Remember also that God refers to Adam as His son, as the beginning of His human family. This means that Abba also regards you as a part of Him because that is how He regards Adam.

One result of our deep and intimate "connectedness" with Abba is that when our thoughts become more like His thoughts, He experiences increased joy. This in a sense is the opposite of what he experienced because of Israel's wickedness as we see in His lament in Isaiah 55:

> *Let the wicked forsake their ways and the unrighteous*
> *their thoughts. Let them turn to the Lord, and he will have*
> *mercy on them, and to our God, for he will freely pardon.*

---

70. See the chapter entitled The Window of Value.

The Window of the Future

"For my thoughts are not your thoughts, neither are your ways my ways," declares the Lord (Isaiah 55:7-8).

But when our thoughts *are* more like His thoughts, He rejoices. A good example is found in David, a man declared by God to be after His own heart.[71] The best example is, of course, Jesus who pleased[72] His Father through His thoughts and attitudes.

Your plans are so precious to Abba that He doesn't require them to be perfect, nor does He summarily thwart them as a matter of practice. Rather, He chooses to guide you in the accomplishment of your (good) objectives:

> *In their hearts humans plan their course, but the Lord determines their steps* (Proverbs 16:9).

> *Trust in the Lord with all your heart and lean not on your own understanding; in all your ways submit to him, and he will make your paths straight* (Proverbs 3:5-6).

Notice that in both of these popular verses, Abba isn't described as necessarily wanting to *cancel* your plans, but rather He (often) helps[73] you along the pathway to achieving them (which can include modification). His love for you is so deep and wide that your joys become *His* joy. Even your plans for accomplishment delight Him before they are accomplished because He anticipates your delight more than you do. As we have noted before, Abba is blessed when *you* are blessed.

Your Heavenly Future Is Precious to Abba

It is very easy to become so preoccupied with our earthly sojourn that we neglect the biggest part of our life—our eternal and exquisite walk with Abba in heavenly realms. His plans for our future are not restricted to our life on earth, even if we think and behave as if they are.

---

71. See 1 Samuel 13:14 and Acts 13:22.

72. See, for example, Matthew 3:17; Mark 1:11; Luke 3:22.

73. For more discussion of Abba's help, see the chapter entitled The Window of Support.

Does He really have specific plans for us in heaven? The apostle Paul makes it clear that the answer is a resounding, "Yes."

> *As it is written: "What no eye has seen, what no ear has heard, and what no human mind has conceived"— the things God has prepared for those who love him— these are the things God has revealed to us by his Spirit* (1 Corinthians 2:9-10).

Notice that Paul declares that the preparations of God for us have been revealed to us by His Spirit.[74] The context refers to the mystery of "God's wisdom, a mystery that has been hidden and that God destined for our glory before time began."[75]

A narrow interpretation of this declaration might focus on the secret wisdom of salvation through the sacrifice of Jesus, but a broader interpretation whets our appetite for the actual reception and understanding of the Spirit's revelation of what is in store for us in heaven. For that, we surely need His help. The question of what awaits us, and in particular what we will be doing in heaven, is huge. This is because its answer is huge; indeed, it is infinite.

In other chapters we will explore a bit more some of the possible things in store for us as we "swim" in the limitless, eternal, blissful sea of relationship with Abba. But for now I hope to simply whet your appetite.

No Harp-Playing on Fluffy White Clouds for Me, Thank You

In days gone by, cartoons frequently depicted the outcome of the death of a character by showing him or her sitting on a fluffy white cloud with a halo above his or her head, harp in hand. This is, of course, a very limited view of our future in heaven. I can imagine becoming excruciatingly bored if I were sitting on a cloud, playing a harp for

---

74. I personally like to regard this as an invitation to go on "field trips" with the Holy Spirit.

75. See 1 Corinthians 2:7.

eternity. If I should find myself in such a state, I would be fairly certain that I went the wrong direction after death—down, and not up.

Kidding aside, I anticipate as a believer the exact *opposite.* I do not expect to be bored in heaven. Abba's desire is that we be continually blessed with discovery of His love, with limitless avenues for expression of creativity, with ever-increasing acquaintance and intimacy with everyone in heaven, and with never-ending enthrallment with His majesty and goodness, to mention just a few.[76] Jesus Himself, echoing the desire of His Father's heart, declared a major part of His purpose on earth:

> *I came that they may have and enjoy life, and have it in abundance [to the full, till it overflows]* (John 10:10b AMP).

The blessings intended for us will be beyond our imagination or our capacity to understand. In one word—limitless.

I Will Want to Get to *Know* You in Heaven, As Well As Possible

Let me illustrate for now just one of the blessings Abba intends for us, and postpone some other examples until later chapters. Many years ago a friend of mine, who was a mature believer, told me that she could hardly wait to get to heaven because then "it will just be me and Jesus." I was actually grieved by that statement because I was thinking, "What about everyone else there in heaven?" I would want to get to know *everyone* in heaven, as well as possible.

Here's why: Everyone in heaven will have my Lord and Lover, Jesus, in them. Each of the sons of God displays Christ in different ways, through expressions of Jesus that are unique to them. Because of my intense desire to know Jesus as well as possible, I will want to get to know *everyone's* expression of Him. In other words, Jesus will show Himself to me in many ways, not the least of which is *through* all my

---

76. I believe that it is not possible to list the thrilling blessings that await us because the list itself would be *infinite.*

brethren, and so I will be intensely motivated to get to know everyone in heaven in my quest to discover as much of Jesus as possible. You will want the same for yourself; how could you not?

This mutual discovery of Jesus in each other is just one example of the blessings that await our oneness in Christ and Him in us. We can whet our appetites for this blessing by looking for Jesus in the eyes of our fellow believers here on earth. I've done this frequently in my own relationships with fellow believers, and every time I've done so I've been blessed by the wonderful and unique expression of Jesus I've seen in each of them. In a sense, we "belong" to each other, and because of that godly, corporate ownership we can expect a unique display of Christ in each of our brothers and sisters that manifests itself as we freely give to one another in love. We can truly say to each other,

"Your expression of Jesus belongs to me, and mine belongs to you."

We can begin the exploration of Jesus in each other now and continue that delight into eternity.

The Window of Eternity

"Father, why did You make time so that it never ends?"

Perhaps because of my previous career as a physicist (researcher and professor), my curiosity sometimes takes forms that may seem a bit strange. I used to study the topics of time and space and many others in the purview of physicists. I tried to find answers to deep questions about the nature of creation by relying on my own intellect and that of gifted scientists and thinkers. Now, because of my relationship with Abba as one of His sons, I can ask Him questions directly and know that He will help me discover answers that aren't suspect because of humanistic philosophies and paradigms.

I was meditating on Abba's creation a few years ago and became focused on the particular part of His creation we call "time." One of my questions that came from that meditation was this:

"Father, why did You make time so that it never ends?"

In other words, I asked Abba to explain to me why eternity exists. The reason why that question even occurred to me was because, from the physicist's point of view, it is possible that time simply "stops" at some point. Einstein's equations forming the backbone of his Theory of General Relativity[77] have possible solutions where time simply ends.[78]

---

77. See, for example, *A Brief History of Time* by Stephen Hawking (New York: Bantam Books, 1988).

78. The conditions for such "time-ceasing" solutions to be applicable seem unlikely now in view of present-day evidence.

I don't mean to imply by this that the physicist's understanding of time is even close to the "reality" created by God, but I'm simply pointing to the fact that it seems possible to man (through man's "wisdom") that time could end.

However, my question was not whether time ends—we know biblically that it does not. We know that His righteousness endures[79] *forever* and that His love endures[80] *forever*. We know that:

> *Heaven and earth will pass away, but my words will never pass away* (Matthew 24:35).

We know that the Lord has "set eternity in the hearts of men."[81] The list of all such Scriptures would be very long indeed.

I knew from God's Word that time would never end; my question for Abba was, "Why? You could have made time so that it ended, but You did not. Why?"

Abba didn't answer me directly; He apparently decided to delegate that delight to the Holy Spirit. The answer I received from the Holy Spirit was clear, concise, and rocked my very soul. Here are the three words He gave me that can be a huge blessing if you will receive them as truth from the Spirit of Truth:

"Love demands eternity."

These three words of revelation will be etched in my consciousness forever. They reveal the immeasurable depth of our loving Father's heart, and I'm convinced that my understanding of the implications of the Holy Spirit's declaration will itself continue to grow on into eternity.

Love demands eternity! Let's unpack some of the biblical foundation for such an amazing declaration. I'm going to share with you the "chain of logic" that convinced me that I had heard the Holy Spirit correctly.

---

79. See for examples: Psalms 111:3 and 112:3, and many other Scriptures.

80. See for examples: 1 Chronicles 16:34; 2 Chronicles 5:13, 7:3; Psalms 100:5; Jeremiah 33:11, and many other Scriptures.

81. See Ecclesiastes 3:11.

You may have your own way of gaining confidence in its truth, but I hope my avenue will, in that event, simply add to your blessing. The following is not meant to be an air-tight proof that I was accurately hearing a declaration by the Holy Spirit but rather a plausible line of reasoning to that end.

First, I think you would agree with me that *God is infinite.* He is beyond measure,[82] beyond understanding,[83] beyond description,[84] inscrutable,[85] limitless,[86] and has no boundary.[87] This infinitude is therefore not restricted to the spatial measures we first consider, but it also applies to many of God's attributes such as limitless wisdom, knowledge, power, and so on. He transcends human effort to arrive at a complete description because He is always more than we have discovered or could discover. It is in this sense that I'm referring to God's infinitude, namely that there is "always more" of Him than we think.

Second, the Bible explicitly declares that *God is love.*[88] This is an incredibly deep statement by the apostle John in its own right, but let's keep on track. Because God is infinite and God is love, we can conclude that *God's love is infinite.*

I think you would agree that *God is good.*[89] Now, because God is good and He is love, you can agree that *His love is good.* Let's summarize:

*God's love is **infinite** and **good**.*

Next, it is important to realize that God withholds no good thing from you:

82. See Lamentations 5:22.

83. See Judges 13:18 and Job 36:26; 37:5.

84. See Romans 11:33.

85. See Isaiah 40:28 (NASB).

86. See John 3:34.

87. See Psalms 119:96.

88. See, for example, 1 John 4:8,16.

89. See, for example, 2 Chronicles 6:41; Psalms 31:19; Galatians 5:22; 2 Timothy 1:5; Titus 3:4; and 2 Peter 1:3.

Windows to the Father's Heart

For the Lord God is a sun and shield; the Lord bestows favor and honor; no good thing does he withhold from those whose walk is blameless (Psalms 84:11).

We arrive now at a key hurdle for most believers. Let me ask this question of you: Do you believe that your walk is blameless? Many of us are tempted to say, "No." That is because we know we are not perfect, but I want to encourage you in this fact: Perfection is not the same as being blameless. This is a truth that needs to be received by every Christian deep within their souls:

> *You have been **made** blameless by the shed blood of Christ.*

Because Jesus took all your blame upon Himself at the cross, God does *not* assign any blame to you whatsoever.[90] Therefore, you are blameless and *God does not withhold any good thing from you.*

It is reasonable to believe that if God's love is good, then the revelation of His love to you is also good.[91] Because it is good, He will not withhold this revelation of His love from you. If I can say it this way:

> *God, being in His very nature love, is **compelled** to reveal His love to you.*

You may object to the statement that God is "compelled" to do anything, but I use that word because I want to emphasize that this compulsion is due to His internal perfection, which exhibits the consistency of His actions with His character. In other words, it is not possible for God to withhold the revelation of His love from you. That is extremely good news.

Now we have arrived at the "punch line," so to speak. Because God's love is infinite, it will take an infinite amount of time for His love to be revealed to you because you are a finite being and cannot absorb or

---

90. See Ephesians 1:3-4.

91. In a sense, the revelation of love is implicit in the nature of love itself.

receive an infinite amount of anything at once. Because God cannot stop revealing His love to you and cannot finish doing so, eternity must exist.

Another way to say this is that if, at some point in the future, God were to "stop time," He would be stopping the revelation of His love to you. He cannot do that, so therefore eternity must exist. We see that our logic can agree with an absolute truth revealed by the Spirit of Truth:

"Love demands eternity."

This answered my question to Abba as to why He made time so that it never ended. But there is more we can glean from this amazing revelation of the necessity of eternity. It may seem rather obvious at this point, but let me highlight a "companion" conclusion that reveals more of Abba's heart. It is this: In order for Abba to reveal His infinite love to you, you must live forever. Or, we can say it a different way:

Because Abba loves you, He was "compelled" to have
you live forever.

You were created to live forever because Abba loves you. Another way to say this is that Abba can never finish loving you.

How Much of Abba's Love Can You Anticipate?

Let's explore another view of this eternally increasing revelation of God's love to you. Consider how much more you feel loved by Abba today than you did, say, one year ago.[92] Now, try to imagine how much more you will feel loved by Abba a million years from now in heaven. If you are like me, my brain starts to fry and smoke may come out of my ears when I try to think about how good that will be. No matter how inadequate my imagination may be in trying to get my brain wrapped around that blessing a million years from now, I do know this—in a million years *plus* one day, the revelation of His love will be even better. Let me summarize this point in a succinct manner:

---

92. If you've only been saved one day, compare today to yesterday.

Windows to the Father's Heart

*Of the **increase** of the revelation of Abba's love there
will be no end.*

My personal opinion is that this point should be made very, very clear when the gospel message is presented to those precious folks who are seeking God. Instead of focusing on what they should be turning *from* (turn or burn evangelism), it is far more attractive to highlight the loving heart they are invited to turn *toward*.

This thought absolutely thrills me—that no matter how much of Abba's love I've been blessed to receive and/or understand at some point in my relationship with Him, there is always an *infinite* amount more that is yet to be discovered and received. This is the nature of infinity—there is *always* more, *infinitely more.* I used to study this intriguing concept from a variety of perspectives in my physics career; now I'm more intrigued than ever before when I apply this concept to God's love—I'm thrilled beyond measure.

The Window of Eternity has this self-evident feature—it will *never* be "shuttered." Moreover, as we will discuss later in more detail, another implication of the existence of eternity is that there are an infinite number of windows. This is but an appetizing glimpse into the infinitely fascinating heart of Abba. We are surely invited to imagine the exquisite delight awaiting us in our eternal relationship with Abba. It requires our spiritual minds be engaged to comprehend, as Paul admonished in 1 Corinthians 2. Even if such comprehension sometimes seems too far out of reach, the blessing to be received is well worth both the choice and the effort to believe that all things are possible.

It is the glory of God to conceal a matter; to search out a matter is the glory of kings (Proverbs 25:2).

The Window of Trust

"Father, why do You trust me with so much?"

Perhaps you may be tempted to ask, as I often am, a different question than that posed here. When I yield to this temptation, I usually ask, "Father, why do You trust me with so *little*?" This is a common temptation, I am sure, but as we gaze through The Window of Trust into Abba's heart, we will discover the amazing riches that motivate Him to trust us. A more accurate question would be, "Father, why do You trust me with *exactly* the right amount?"

"Are You sure this is the right amount, Abba?"

Let's begin by viewing the parable of the talents[93] (or bags of gold) from two points of view—our human perspective and Abba's loving perspective. Assuming you've read that passage of Scripture, let me just quote the first two verses:

> *Again, it [the kingdom of heaven] will be like a man going on a journey, who called his servants and* ***entrusted*** *his wealth to them. To one he gave five bags of gold, to another two bags, and to another one bag,* ***each according to his ability*** *(Matthew 25:14-15).*

There is an uncountable number of sermons based on this parable. It is rich with lessons, and many of them could spawn additional chapters

---

93. See Matthew 25:14-30.

in this book, but let's focus on these first two verses and their insight into Abba's heart.

The man (or master) who goes on a journey represents Jesus ascending after His resurrection, with an implied eventual return, and the servants represent His disciples. The fact that He entrusts us (His disciples) with *anything* of value is itself remarkable, at least at first glance. In doing so, He echoes Abba's belief in us that, in spite of our imperfections, we do have the ability to multiply the value of that with which we have been entrusted. With the help of the Holy Spirit, much can be accomplished that we may not even believe can be done at the outset of our stewardship.

What sorts of "valuables" might we be entrusted with? The list is very long indeed. Here are just a few:

- *Time*
- *Treasure (money)*
- *Free will*
- *Earth and its inhabitants*
- *Relationships*
- *Talents/Skills*
- *Children*
- *Destinies*
- *Revelation(s)*
- *Spiritual gifts*
- *Kingdom advancement*

As you can imagine, many sermons could be preached about any of these "treasures" in particular. But let's look from more global or general perspectives concerning the *essence* of what Abba is revealing through The Window of Trust about His heart toward us.

The fact that Abba delegates treasures to our care is first made clear[94] after He created Adam and Eve and charged them with the rule (or loving stewardship) of the earth and its inhabitants. Did He *need* to have the help of man to take care of the earth? Of course not. Rather

---

94. See Genesis 1:26, 28.

than create man in order to help the Godhead take care of the earth, He presumably had other motive(s). The revelation of His motives might just require eternity for its completion, but we can speculate based on Abba's heart of love for His creation, *adam*.[95]

We find a clue to Abba's motive a little further along in the parable of the talents (bags of gold). The first two servants, having both been diligent to double their *different* amounts of their master's money that had been entrusted to them, received exactly the *same* praise upon his return:

> *Well done, good and faithful servant! You have been faithful with a few things; I will put you in charge of many things. Come and share your master's happiness!* (Matthew 25:21 and 23)

There is abundant speculation concerning what exactly constitutes the master's happiness (or "joy" in some translations), but we can infer at the very least that Abba wants to reward us by multiplying our joy when we multiply the delight of His Son.

In addition, sharing with Jesus in Abba's happiness implies an exquisite communion with their hearts. On one hand, it is important to recognize that part of this shared joy has to do with seeing "fruit" from our labors. For example, we gain a sense of satisfaction from the production of more good from something that is itself good. Recall from the chapter entitled The Window of Value that God Himself was pleased with His creation and we, being made in His image, can also be delighted with what we produce, create, or multiply.

There is a much deeper joy that is our reward, however. This is the joy that we share with Jesus because of the pleasure Abba Himself receives as a result of our growth as His sons and daughters. This pleasure engendered in Abba's heart is not so much derived from our expended effort in its own right but instead is the result of how we are

---

95. As stated before, we mean the *entire* race or family called *adam*.

changed in the process. This general concept will be discussed in The Window of Joy, but for now we can perhaps summarize it as follows:

Abba delights when His trust in us bears the fruit of our increased Christlikeness.

It is this perspective from Abba's heart that greatly magnifies our joy, because we are blessed when He is blessed. As our hearts become one with His, we experience more of His joy. All that He has (including His joy) becomes progressively ours[96] as we become more like Jesus.

It is important to note that our *approach* to the lesson(s) contained in the parable of the talents (bags of gold) can greatly affect the nature of our reward. Specifically, I have in mind the contrast between regarding Abba's entrustments as necessitating a *dutiful response* on our part as compared with the excitement (and even thrill) of regarding these entrustments as *opportunities* to bless our Father, as we submit to the process of the Holy Spirit developing Christlikeness in our character and attitudes. The former approach characterizes the approach of a *servant* fulfilling his duty while the latter exemplifies the anticipation of a *son* who rejoices in being about his Father's business.

Our perceptions of Abba's entrustment are usually subject to our soulish filters. For example, when it comes to money I often think I'm entrusted with too little. When I consider responsibility, I instead think I'm entrusted with too much. There are many other examples of our mistaken perception. It's only when I view Abba's trust in me from the perspective of His amazing love that I begin to apprehend the perfection of His assessment of my ability to steward His treasures appropriately.

The right amount of entrustment by Abba is inextricably tied to our own individual and unique abilities, not because He wants to load us up with the maximum we can handle without keeling over in exhaustion with our efforts to keep up our "performance," but rather because He knows exactly how to ensure our success (with His help)

---

96. The kingdom *has already been* given to us by the Father (see Luke 12:32), but our reception and occupation of the kingdom is progressive in many respects.

that will in turn give us a sense of accomplishment that is not "too easy" and hence less fulfilling when completed.

This perfect entrustment is also motivated by His intense desire to nurture His sons into maturity or, in other words, into Christlikeness.[97] Although He personally knows how much we can handle and how much will stretch us appropriately, we do not. As Abba progressively prepares us for more responsibility, He follows His perfect design of the process itself so that we learn along the way just how wonderfully capable He has made us, while at the same time teaching us to rely totally on the Holy Spirit for His perfect guidance.

A simple illustration may help us to appreciate this point. When a father begins to teach his son how to ride a bicycle, there may be reluctance on the part of his son because he thinks he "can't do it." Yet the father knows when his child is ready to learn, and he gently encourages the skittish novice with expressions of loving trust, such as, "Yes, you can, son; I believe in you. I know you can do it; let's try together and I'll help you."

This example illustrates one of the reasons why Abba entrusts expanded responsibility to us at successive stages along our path of maturity: He wants us to learn to "ride the bike" and, more importantly, to learn through the present lesson in which we are "immersed" that we can probably do even much more with His help. Each time we steward a responsibility well, we can expect to be entrusted with more, as the parable promises. This becomes very exciting when we consider its continuance escalating into eternity.

Experience Is Essential

We can only learn such lessons by our own experience and not solely by that of others. This means we have to be careful not to fall victim to the deception that vicarious training is preferable or even possible. For example, it's hard to learn how to ride a bicycle by simply watching a friend ride one or by watching Internet tutorial videos. Put another way, I'm pretty sure you would not want to be a passenger on a jet whose

97. See, for example, Romans 8:29.

pilot had never actually flown a real plane, but had only spent many (perhaps even hundreds of) hours in a flight simulator. Yikes.

Let's examine a powerful lesson from the story of Abraham's response to God's command to sacrifice his son Isaac.[98] When God asked Abraham to take his only son Isaac to a particular mountaintop and sacrifice him, Abraham must surely have wondered why he was being asked to do such a thing. Yet, as we know from the story, he set out in obedience early the next morning with Isaac to carry out this extremely disturbing task. God's last-second interruption of Abraham's obedient thrust of a knife into Isaac's heart on the makeshift mountaintop altar was presumably already planned. What was God's point in testing Abraham this way?

We may not be able to understand this in full measure, but I think it is fair to say that one component of God's purpose was to reveal to Abraham that he (Abraham) could even be obedient to carry out such a horrific task. Perhaps this "test" or "proving" was for Abraham's sake, not necessarily God's alone.

Another way to view the blessing of such testing is that God's trust in you is interwoven with your trust in Him. Abraham reasoned that God could somehow restore Isaac back to life, so that He could fulfill His promise to Abraham that Isaac would have nations come from his loins. God trusted Abraham to be obedient, and Abraham trusted God to provide a solution so that the promise could be fulfilled. The result? God was assured that his trust in Abraham was well founded[99] and Abraham was assured that his trust in God was well founded.[100] Their relationship was powerfully strengthened through this experience.

An additional lesson from this example is that when we ask Abba to show us more of His heart, He may answer by arranging circumstances so that we experience some of His heart.[101] That is because He knows

---

98. See Genesis 22:1-18.

99. See Genesis 22:12.

100. See Hebrews 11:19.

101. See the warning in The Window of Choice that says the process of learning about Abba's heart is not just *observational* but *participatory*.

best, of course, how to teach us. In the present context, we see that trust is fortified through experience of faithfulness.

Say Goodbye to Comparison

It is wise as we grow in trustworthiness to be careful to not imagine ourselves superior to others because our same-age friend Johnny is still at tricycle stage and we are riding a bicycle now, nor to imagine ourselves inferior because our other same-age friend Tommy is already mastering the unicycle. It may be relatively easy to catch ourselves in the first comparison (with Johnny) because we can quickly recognize that thought as a manifestation of pride. However, it may not be so obvious to us that in the second comparison (with Tommy) our feeling of inferiority is also a manifestation of pride, even though it may appear to be jealousy at first glance.

Let me explain. There are perhaps thousands of pulpits from which it is taught that it is important to keep oneself humble by declaring that "I'm just a sinner, saved by grace," or "I'm just a worm," or "I'm just a vapor," or "I'm worthless without Jesus," and so on in like manner. The goal in such teachings is to encourage the listener to remain humble and not get too puffed up with pride. However, in my opinion all such mandated declarations are lies from the pit of hell and are, if truly believed by the person professing one or more of them, evidence of false humility.

When we declare or even think things about ourselves along the lines of these examples, we are essentially disagreeing with Abba who proclaims quite the contrary about His sons and daughters. For example, we are "more than conquerors,"[102] "able to do all things through Christ who strengthens" us,[103] for whom "all things are possible" if we believe,[104] who give "great delight"[105] to our Abba, and whom Abba

---

102. See Romans 8:37.

103. See Philippians 4:13.

104. See Mark 9:23.

105. See Zephaniah 3:17.

regards as the "apple(s) of his eye."[106] The list of such declarations by God is quite long indeed.

When we disagree in this way with Abba, we have provided evidence that we value our own opinions of ourselves more highly than His opinion of us. Regarding our own thoughts as more important than God's is a clear manifestation of pride. When we deceive ourselves into thinking we are humble by disagreeing with Abba, we can expect our loving Father to discipline us with the goal of delivering our minds from such garbage.

It is best for us to simply agree with Abba concerning ourselves:

*True humility is evidenced by **agreement** with God.*

Be encouraged that the amount or nature of what you have been entrusted with is precisely the appropriate measure for you and has nothing to do with the amount entrusted to someone else. Abba's trust in you is perfect because it is an expression of His perfect love for you.

---

106. See Deuteronomy 32:10 and Zechariah 2:8.

The Window of Support

"Father, can I count on Your support?"

D o you know that your Abba is *eager* to strongly support you? I used to wonder about this for many years. In my Bible reading I invariably encountered this verse that haunted me:

For the eyes of the Lord run to and fro throughout the whole earth, to give strong support to those whose heart is blameless toward him. (2 Chronicles 16:9a ESV).

Whenever I read this verse I felt dismayed because I believed that I didn't really qualify for the blessing of His strong support. Why? Because I knew that my heart wasn't always perfect toward my Father in heaven. I could have made a long list of the times when I didn't even think about Him because I was wrapped up in my busyness, distractions, sinful thought patterns, or worse yet when I was angry with Him because He hadn't done what I wanted.

Because of my self-disqualification, I often felt like Abba's eyes went right past me on His searches of the earth without even a second glance to consider me again for this blessing. On some occasions, however, when I was feeling better about my standing with Abba, I would at least attempt to "get His attention" when I imagined His eyes about to pass me by, much in the same way someone stranded on a desert island might try to get the attention of a rescue plane or ship passing in the distance by waving, shouting, or building a fire.

Windows to the Father's Heart

"Look at me, Daddy. Here I am. Can I count on Your support?"

But that time would pass and I would feel once again that His eyes had passed me by. I tried to forget the disappointment until the next time I read through the Bible and encountered that inescapable, dreaded verse.

Yes, there is a *good* end to this story. A few years ago, I was dragging my heart through this same verse yet again and I (as expected) felt disqualified for Abba's support. I wanted to skip the verse altogether, but I had committed to reading the *entire* Bible every other year, something I had done without fail for decades. I couldn't reach my disciplined goal that year if I skipped over some verses I didn't really like or found less interesting than others (like genealogies, for example).

But this time, God spoke to me clearly, saying,

"Son, My eyes have stopped searching; I've found you."

Wow! I could hardly believe my ears. Fortunately, I've learned to try to resist the temptation to respond by asking this all-too-common, and frankly nonsensical, question: "Are You sure, Abba?" Instead, I tried to understand how it could be that His statement might possibly be consistent with what I "knew" about myself as a result of frequently swimming in the sea of self-disqualification.

The only way I could see any consistency with what this verse gave as a condition for Abba's strong support and what I heard His voice telling me was that somehow my heart was "blameless toward Him." How could this be? Surely, it wasn't possible for me to have a perfect heart toward Abba because I knew my heart was imperfect—it was desperately wicked and full of deceit.[107]

I felt the nudge of the Holy Spirit guiding me into more truth. Abba didn't require my heart to be perfect but just blameless in order to show Himself strong in my behalf. Here is the wonderful truth about our hearts if we have received salvation through faith in Christ:

---

107. See Jeremiah 17:9.

The Window of Support

*Our hearts have been made **blameless** by the blood of the Lamb.*

Christ took all blame upon Himself at the cross. There is none left for us! Abba assigns no blame to us and specifically none to our hearts whatsoever. This a corollary of the good news that even though we may be tempted to assign blame to our own hearts, perhaps in agreement with Satan, our accuser, it is a fact that Abba assigns none to us.[108] For this reason, I can confidently encourage every saint to consider his or her heart blameless toward Abba and as a result to begin to *expect* His strong support.

*Abba's eyes have stopped searching—they are fixed on **you**.*

Abba has arranged for your heart to satisfy His condition for showing Himself strong in your behalf. There is not any other thing you must do in order to qualify for this blessing—it is yours[109] because of the sacrifice of Jesus in obedience to His Father.

Remember what was pointed out in The Window of Eternity—namely, that Abba withholds no good thing from him whose walk is blameless.[110] Abba's display of strong support for you is a good thing, so you can grow to expect strong, even outrageous support from Him. How can I say outrageous support is yours from Abba? Because for God, "strong support" is ridiculously beyond all we can think or ask.[111] If Abba is for you, who can be against you?[112]

Let's take this a little further, as we look more deeply into the Father's heart through this window. Even if you've been taught, in the name of reverence and humility, to believe that God somehow tolerates

---

108. See Romans 8:1.
109. See Ephesians 1:3-4.
110. See Psalms 84:11c.
111. See Ephesians 3:20.
112. See Romans 8:31.

you or even perhaps lovingly just waits to fix problems that arise in your life, I am compelled by the love of Christ to tell you the truth:

*Abba is not only **willing** to strongly support you, He is **eager** to do so.*

Your Abba is not just occupied with cleaning up your messes; He is excited about strongly supporting you in your adventures with Him.

The Elephant and the Mouse

I often like to tell the fable I heard long ago[113] about the elephant and the mouse in Africa who were best friends. These two buddies did everything together and were rarely seen very far from one another. They learned a great deal about how things appear to someone who is large compared to the viewpoint of someone small. And they learned to increasingly value these different perspectives as they "did life together" as best friends. Theirs was a friendship that many other animals said must have been forged in heaven because of the vast difference in their perspectives.

Although it was difficult for the elephant to get "low enough" to the ground to gain the perspective of his friend the mouse, it was often the case that the mouse would hitch a ride on the elephant's head and have the delightful treat of a much higher perspective along their shared paths in the jungle. The elephant didn't seem to mind this imbalance because he loved his friend, the mouse, and often protected him from harm or assisted him with difficult tasks that required far more strength than the little mouse had.

The mouse in turn often made the elephant laugh because of his playfulness and antics as he scampered along. This little friend often invited avoidable trouble through his explorations of their vast jungle world but always trusted his big buddy, the elephant, to rescue him. The other animals often counseled the elephant to be careful with how much he allowed the mouse to impose on his big heart, presuming on

---

113. I've forgotten from whom I first heard this fable. My apologies for that *and* for any embellishments I can't resist.

his protection, but the elephant didn't mind at all because of his love for his friend.

One very windy day, however, it was the mouse's turn to help his friend. They were enjoying their customary fellowship along a path in the jungle when all of a sudden they were startled to see other animals running past them as fast as they could. "Run for your lives. Run for your lives," the animals said. "The fire is coming fast." Soon they could see the flames in the distance, leaping very fast along the tops of trees in the stiff wind. They needed to find a way to outrun the fire.

Their escape was complicated by the simultaneous advance of another fire also advancing rapidly toward them along the only escape path known by the elephant to be big enough for him to travel. Escape seemed hopeless to the elephant. But the mouse jumped down to the ground from his perch on the elephant's head and yelled, "Follow me. I know a way that might work." The elephant had newfound gratitude for the mouse's many explorations of the jungle.

While the mouse was able to easily scamper along the trail, running along fallen logs and zigzagging around many small trees, the elephant out of necessity had to travel a more direct path, pushing over the small trees in the way as he tried to keep up with the mouse. At times the elephant had to push with all his might to break the trees in his way, but he was highly motivated to do so. They had to keep running—the fire was gaining on them.

All of a sudden they reached a river in a very deep and steep ravine. The elephant exclaimed in fright, "I can't jump down there. I'll die for sure if I try." The mouse, however, knew there was a bridge spanning across the ravine not too far away and said, "Hurry, follow me. There is a bridge over there, but we have to hurry. The fire is close now; the bridge is our only chance."

They reached the bridge with the fire right behind them, but the elephant was further panicked because the bridge was made of only ropes and planks and looked very old and rickety. He thought, This may be safe for a mouse, or a person perhaps, but for a big guy like me?

Yikes. The mouse shouted again, "Let's go across. It's our only chance." They had to cross right then, or jump, or be burned alive.

The mouse went first, running easily across the bridge. The elephant followed as fast as he could. As he did, the ropes were breaking and planks were falling into the river far below. Behind him the bridge was no more, much like a scene out of an Indiana Jones movie.[114] Somehow, the elephant made it all the way across, with the remnant of the bridge now uselessly slapping in the wind against the side of the ravine.

"Whew." They both let out sighs of relief, and gave thanks that their lives were spared in the nick of time. The fire on the other side of the ravine had now consumed everything up to the edge. Once they managed to catch their breath, the mouse turned to the elephant and said,

"Wow, we really made that bridge shake, didn't we?"

The elephant just smiled as he replied to his little friend, "Yep, we sure did."

Although there are a few lessons we could explore from this fable, let me focus on the heart of the elephant toward his friend after they reached safety and the mouse claimed some "out-sized" credit for shaking the bridge. Even though the elephant's weight and power far exceeded that of the mouse, he lovingly allowed the mouse to claim a disproportionate share of the credit for shaking the bridge. This is how I often feel when Abba shows Himself strong on my behalf. He is the elephant[115] and I'm the mouse. He is eager to back me up and support me. He encourages me with a glorifying pat on the back, saying, "Good job, son. I'm proud of you." This in spite of the fact that all the power to get the job done came from Him in the first place!

"My Daddy Can Do Anything."

As sons we can expect "outrageous" support from Abba when we are "about His business." In my ministry in both Africa and North America

---

114. This is a fable, remember.

115. At other times, the elephant's role is a representation of the help given by the Holy Spirit or Jesus in my adventures with God.

over a period of many years, I've often found myself in seemingly impossible situations that require miraculous solutions. I've recorded the testimonies of several of these in some of my audio messages, but let me focus here on just one to give you the flavor of this lesson about Abba's heart. My hope is that you will be encouraged to adopt this key to seeing the "impossible" happen right before *your* eyes. My intent with this example is not to boast about what I've seen, but rather to encourage you to believe that Abba wants to strongly support *you*.

In the early days of my African ministry, I had only been home a couple of days from a short-term mission trip to Tanzania when I received an e-mail from my bishop friend who had hosted and arranged my ministry visit there the week before. He wrote that a wonderful Christian friend of his, who lived a fair distance from his village, had arrived at his home too late to meet me; I had already left on my journey home. The man was discouraged because he had hoped to meet me in person to present a request for financial assistance in connection with his own ministry to blind children.

This Christian man had such a heart of compassion for blind children that he often traveled to several scattered locations to meet at various times, individually, with about a dozen of them in total to encourage them and help with some of their needs as best he could. It was beyond his means to provide essential items such as Braille learning materials and books, as well as help with support for their guardians, parents, or caring friends.[116] He needed money, and lots of it, in order to adequately help these children.

I was moved by this man's compassion for the blind children and wrote back to the bishop saying that I could send a little money now. I strongly encouraged the bishop to pray for those children that they would be healed of blindness—not only would that be the very best way to help them, but it was also a *lot cheaper*. I wrote that, in the event that

---

116. One blind child was so shunned by villagers, who thought he was demonically cursed, that he spent most of every day in a cave and only under cover of night was helped by a compassionate friend who led him to a safe hut on the outskirts of the village to sleep with his family.

some of them were not healed by the time of my next visit (in about five months) I would also like to pray with the children in person for their healing, adding my prayers to the bishop's own.

I didn't receive any more news about these children until I arrived at the bishop's village five months later. He had prayed for them from his own prayer closet since he was unable to carve out enough time from his busy schedule (overseeing about two dozen widely scattered churches) to personally visit the children. I found out that none of them had yet been healed, so the Christian man planned on bringing them all to the bishop's village to meet with me in person so that I could pray for them, as I had promised.

Sure enough, near the end of the Sunday morning service at the bishop's church where I was preaching, I saw about a dozen blind children entering the back of the church with their caretakers or parents, quietly taking seats at the rear of the congregation. I knew that they had come to receive healing ministry and I was extremely eager to pray for them. But at the end of the service I was instead escorted out a side door and led to the bishop's home for lunch. This is the custom in East Africa—namely, to make sure the visiting man of God is honored and cared for (in this case with food) and not imposed upon too much by others.

That lunch seemed to take *forever*. Visitor after visitor came to the bishop's home to greet me and discuss urgent matters with me during the prolonged lunchtime. Finally, about four o'clock in the afternoon, we finished and I was escorted on our short walk back to the church so that I could pray with the children who had evidently been waiting patiently for three more hours while I had some lunch. I was excited to at last be able to pray with them.

On that short walk to the church to pray with the children, I suddenly had an almost overwhelming thought about the possible outcome of this impending ministry: *What if it doesn't work? There is a room full of blind children expecting **me** to do something about their condition, to get them healed.* I was feeling enormous pressure to perform miracles.

90

I quickly realized that the question, "What if it doesn't work?" was a thought birthed in doubt and not from God.

I took authority over this thought from the pit of hell and commanded it to depart from my mind. Then I proclaimed out loud, with forcefulness, that

"My Daddy can do anything."

At the very instant that I spoke those words out loud, the doubt left my mind. I was free to believe with certainty that those children would be healed. In my mind was rock-solid belief that the miracles so desperately hoped for by these children would in fact be accomplished by my Abba through His support of my efforts to carry out His business. I had exchanged the reliance on my own inability for the far superior reliance on His ability. This is the key that I mentioned above:

*I traded my **inability** for His **ability**.*

Once I had made this exchange, I knew the children would be healed. I just didn't know exactly how.

"Ask for the Toughest Case."

As we entered the church full of blind children (about a dozen), their caretakers, several pastors, and other assorted onlookers, I simply asked Holy Spirit, "How do You want me to proceed? What is Your strategy?" I was a bit taken aback, but not really surprised, when Holy Spirit replied, *"Ask for the toughest case."* I must confess that at that point I wondered why I couldn't just be allowed to "warm up" on someone with slightly blurry vision. But I knew my Abba had sent that advice through Holy Spirit, so I would be well advised to follow His instruction.

I asked, and they brought me the toughest case—a young girl about eight or nine years old, a precious and beautiful girl who had been completely blind since birth. As they stood her about three feet in front of me, I asked another question of Holy Spirit: "How do You want me to pray?"[117] He replied instantly, "Cast out the spirit of infirmity."[118] I did just that, commanding with authority[119] in Jesus' name the spirit of infirmity to leave her immediately and never return.

I then tested the effectiveness of that command by asking the girl, through the interpreter, to walk over to a spot I pointed to about ten feet away. The interpreter conveyed my request in Kiswahili, and the girl obediently walked over to the spot I had pointed to, even easily negotiating a step down along the way to get to a lower level of the floor. She could see. Praise God for His incredible mercy on her.

The place went *nuts*. By that I mean everyone who witnessed this miracle cried out and jumped up and down with joy. Even the other blind children were clapping and laughing once they understood what had happened to the girl. My friend the bishop was actually jumping and twirling in the air as he shouted for joy.

I was actually surprised by the exuberance of the joy and praise. I had seen many blind people healed before, and so had the bishop and many of the pastors who were present. The level of celebration seemed incommensurate with the miracle. It was as if Jesus had come back. I was rejoicing, but I was puzzled by the eruption of such incredible joy. My bishop friend took one look at my puzzled face and came over to me to help me understand. He said, "*Rafiki*,[120] I can see that you are somehow confused. Let me explain. You had no way of knowing this, but the girl was also *deaf*."

Wow. She had *heard* the request of the interpreter in her native language of Kiswahili, which she had learned a little of before she became deaf at the age of two. She was healed of *deafness* as well as *blindness* when I cast out the spirit of infirmity. Praise the Holy Spirit for His simple advice to me on how to pray. If I had proceeded along the lines that I might have followed on my own, then I might have missed the opportunity to see her completely healed of the deafness I

---

117. Asking this question is another extremely important key for effective prayer ministry.

118. See Matthew 10:8.

119. See Luke 10:19.

120. The Kiswahili word for "friend" is *rafiki*.

didn't even know about, unless someone eventually told me about that condition as well.

"Downhill from Here"

That support from Abba was very welcome indeed. But it doesn't end there. The faith of everyone present was catapulted into the stratosphere, so to speak. The next child they brought to me was a boy, who had also been completely blind since birth. When I prayed for him, his eyes were "opened." Hallelujah! The next child in line was also a boy, completely blind from birth, but unfortunately his father who came with him would not let us pray for his son in the name of Jesus because of his own religious opposition to Christianity. I found out later that the father of this blind boy thought he was coming to a meeting to receive financial assistance for his son.

Even after the bishop and pastors shed tears as they begged the father to let me pray for healing of his son, he would not give assent. This refusal came on the heels of watching two children completely healed in front of him. This was appalling to me and to everyone else present in the church. I don't pray in any other name, so this presented a big problem. The leaders finally gave up and gave the father some money to help him, and he went on his way with his still-blind son.[121]

Even though that fiasco was extremely disheartening to all of us, we continued the ministry to the remaining blind children, who had varying degrees of visual impairment. All of them were healed. The joy level was tremendous, and with powerfully increased faith, the caretakers and parents also asked[122] for healing prayer and they were also completely healed. Praise the Lord!

Abba's strong support that Sunday afternoon as an entire room full of blind children and caretakers were healed (except the one boy whose

121. As the boy and his father walked out of the church and while we were yet shedding tears of disappointment, I made an urgent, silent appeal to Abba, saying, "Someday, Father, I want to see that boy again, and more importantly I want him to *see* me." I believe that our paths will cross again, and that boy will see me with healed eyes.

122. Interestingly, virtually all of the caretakers or parents had some sort of physical problem, including tumors, arthritis pain, fevers, back pain, and so on. *All* were healed. Praise the Lord!

father refused prayer) showed us all that He is full of compassion and mercy toward the sick and infirm. I do not know whether all those blind children previously believed in Jesus as their Savior and Lord, but I do know that Abba was *eager* to heal them that day as we ministered His love.

This example is but one of many that I (and many others) could share about Abba's strong support for His sons as they carry out His displays of lovingkindness. But I want to refresh the focus alluded to above:

*Your Abba wants you to **expect** Him to "back you up."*

There is nothing too hard for God. When you truly believe that He will back you up in what would otherwise be impossible situations, you will be emboldened to imagine, and even expect, unlimited support from Abba. I encourage you to think big and remember that:

All things are possible to him who believes (Mark 9:23 NASB).

I further encourage you to take a moment to write down at least three outrageous things that you would like to do with your Abba's help. And I do mean "outrageous." He is "able to do immeasurably more than all we ask or imagine, according to his power that is at work within us" (Ephesians 3:20).

The Window of Affection

"Father, how do You show Your affection for me?"

A very curious thing began to happen in my life in May of 1998, and it is ongoing even as I write this eighteen years later. "Thing" is a grossly insufficient label for the relentless pursuit of Abba after my heart that I have experienced. Please allow me to share the short version of this very long but fascinating saga, because it provides an amazing window into Abba's heart. The sheer length of this encounter is actually part of the message.

Daily Mystery

Sometime in May 1998 I became aware of a daily mysterious communication from God that I did not understand for about two and a half years until the revelation finally hit me. I began to see the number "444" every day, at least once, and often twice or even three or more times. I saw it on my watch, on clocks, on the cycle display at my gym, on the license plates of cars in front of me on the road, in phone numbers, on billboards, on receipts at Starbucks, bus route numbers, street addresses, time stamps on e-mails, new credit card numbers, music track lengths on CDs, and more. I wasn't looking for appearances of 444; I was mystified by these surprising "pop-ups."

Strange? Yes, indeed. But what made it even more unusual was that one of my best friends began seeing it also in May 1998, every day, at least once if not more. He lived in another city in California, having recently moved away that same month from my town, and we discovered

95

this commonality when we happened to meet again for a ministry event a few months into our "adventure." We were surprised, to say the least, when we both had the same "news" to share—namely, seeing the number 444 every day, without fail, and with the same (approximate, if not *exact*) start date for the "sightings," shortly after he had moved with his wife to their new home about ninety minutes' drive away.

My friend and I often had similar supernatural experiences over the years, including visions, dreams, and prophetic words, so the fact that we both shared this new, albeit bizarre, experience was not altogether surprising when we remembered the other similarities we had already experienced. Many of these were well known to our mutual friends, and we were often referred to as "twins in the Spirit." Even strangers sometimes asked if we were brothers.

By the time we got together in late July of 1998 and discovered our mutual mystery, we had both searched the Scriptures, looking for clues regarding what this particular number might mean. We knew that God was communicating something important to us, but what? The number 444 is not explicitly in the text of the Bible, but there are several interesting occurrences of the word "four" appearing three times in a verse or short passage. There are also several verses with the address 4:44 or 44:4. In the first months of 444 sightings, we had independently studied these verses, written detailed notes, prayed much, and tried to find some meaning to this daily barrage of 444. We continued to pray and seek counsel. Some possibilities emerged, and friends continued to offer interpretations, but we had no clear revelation for a long time. The meaning remained a mystery.

We both wondered if God was trying to warn us about something because of the relentless insistence of this number invading our daily lives. Was God's insistence due to our thick skulls? Did He have something urgent to tell us? Was there a disaster coming? Was there a calamity coming on April 4, 2004 (04/04/04)? "Father, do I only have six years to live? If so, what about my good friend? Are we both coming home to heaven on that day?" It would be difficult to list all the strange thoughts that occurred to us as we groped in the dark.

God Spoke through an Answering Machine?

After about five months of this puzzling daily 444 blitz, we had a joint encounter with God's seeming urgency about this number. We lived in different towns, and he had occasion to be back in my town on a Wednesday for a work-related task and mentioned that he would love to come to my place for a visit in the afternoon after finishing his work.

I lived at that time in a simple back-house in Redondo Beach, California, and my friend arrived in mid-afternoon. We enjoyed catching up on news items, not the least of which was our continued mutual but independent daily sightings of 444. During our conversation, the power in my back-house suddenly shut off. This wasn't a surprise to me, however, because my entire unit was connected to just one circuit that was also shared by the single mom and her daughter who lived in the front house. Often there was an overload on the circuit when our multiple appliances were in use, so I was used to having to take a short walk to the circuit breaker box on the outside wall of the front house to flip the breaker back on.

I excused myself from my conversation with my friend to go flip the breaker switch, but before I reached my door to walk to the front house, the power came back on by itself. I looked at the breaker box on the front house wall and no one was around. I surmised that there must have been a general neighborhood power outage and the power was now restored without the circuit breaker. Fine, no problem. I came back to my living room to talk with my buddy, but first I stopped by the answering machine on my desk to reinitialize it after the power loss. (It had an all-too-familiar light flashing: "PL.")

When I punched a button on my machine to find out what time the loss occurred, my machine spoke in a familiar mechanical monotone: "Four forty-four." Startled, I asked my friend, "Did you hear that?" He hadn't paid attention, so I hit the button again. "Four forty-four," said the mechanical voice. This time he heard it, and we both fell prostrate on the floor, trembling and knowing for sure that God was responsible for the power loss and was now speaking this number to us both.

The presence of God was thick now in my living room and we were convinced that God was serious about getting a message through to us. That was the only afternoon that my friend and I were ever both together in the afternoon at 4:44 p.m., and apparently God chose that singular occasion to speak the mysterious 444 to us together.

Finally, the Revelation of Meaning

I have many other rather crazy 444 stories[123] that I've accumulated over the years of this relentless daily encounter, but let me get to the main point. After many months (approximately two and a half *years*) of these daily 444 sightings, I was finally blessed by Abba with the revelation of what was going on. By revelation from the Holy Spirit, I learned that Abba was *not* trying to warn me about something, and He was not alluding to some cryptic meaning[124] in the number itself. Rather,

*Abba was giving me daily **kisses**.*

Yes, the mystery had an incredibly simple resolution. But the blessings have gone far beyond just the resolution of a mystery; there are multiple expressions of endearment and love notes in the many thousands of "kisses" from Abba that I've received over these eighteen years[125] through this particular mode of affection.

Most of the time I see 444 I feel affection from Abba. It's very simple and tender. On some occasions, I feel as though He is saying "Atta, boy," or "Good job, son," or "You are on the right track; keep going." Sometimes, He confirms my crazy story *during* my telling. For

123. I shared some of the stories from the first seven years in a conference message I delivered in October 2005 entitled, "Encounters of the 444th Kind," which is available as an MP3 audio recording by visiting our ministry website at www.fatherstouch.org/store. There is a "surprise" near the end of the message, so be sure to listen to the end. If you are reading this book far into the future from 2016 and this website is long gone, then you may have to track down a copy of the audio recording using your prophetic gifting. Go on a treasure hunt. ☺

124. Several of my friends graciously offered various possible meanings or interpretations of the number 444 and these possibilities are interesting and perhaps relevant for other saints or for the body of Christ as a whole.

125. I haven't been in as frequent touch with my friend these last few years, but at last check-in he was also still seeing 444 very often.

example, I was sharing the 444 saga with a good friend of mine during a coffee meeting many years ago at a hotel restaurant. He had ordered a latte and I had a simple cup of their house coffee. He graciously picked up the tab and I was with him when the cashier rang up the total at the counter. Yep, you guessed it: $4.44. I exclaimed, "Did you see that total?" (He wasn't paying attention as he was talking with another of our friends during checkout.) He said, "No, what is it?" When I showed him the receipt the cashier was handing him, he stood in awe, exclaiming, "I'm beginning to see what you mean."

This sort of confirmation happens often, but I want to focus on sharing some of the endearment of Abba's heart to me when He encourages me at decision times. For example, I may be driving my car and pondering a decision I need to make: Should I choose A or should I choose B? Which is the best, Abba? A or B? I hope it's A; I think it's A; yep, I'll choose A. Just then, a car may drive by me in the next lane on the highway, with a license plate that contains 444. Coincidence? I don't think so. It's A. Done deal.

At other times, when I have finished a difficult task or project and am wondering if the work was done in a spirit of excellence (my preference), just then it is often the case that I will see 444, which in such cases means Abba is saying to me, "Good job, son. Well done." He is reassuring me.

On the other hand, if I am wondering if I may have taken the wrong fork in the road, so to speak, a 444 sighting tells me that Abba is affirming that I'm on the right track instead. This has happened countless times in the last eighteen years.

How do I know all these "kisses" are from Abba? Most of the time, I hear Him call me "Son" in the process of my being "kissed"—"I love you, son." Those are the most common words I hear. Even as I'm writing this chapter, I'm overwhelmed by His affection for me. Abba's love is real; it is tangible; it is *life*.

Why did Abba choose 444 as the "carrier" of His affection to me? I don't know for sure, but I do know that I've been trained as a scientist to spot patterns of various kinds in a variety of situations and circumstances, and numbers catch my attention. More generally, I believe that Abba selected a love language that He knew would be just right for me. Nevertheless, I've learned from several of my spiritual children that they are seeing 444 often also; some are seeing it every day. Apparently this phenomenon can be contagious. Rarely does a day go by now that I don't have a 444 sighting report from at least one of my spiritual children. I don't count those 444s, however, as my personal kisses from Abba; I know at least one is coming that day to me *personally*.

Abba Is Relentless

A conservative calculation tells me that, at a bare minimum, I've been "kissed" by Abba with 444 at least 6,500 times since I first became aware of it in 1998. The actual number is much higher because most days I experience two or more kisses. So, I think it is fair to say I've now been kissed, by the time of this writing, about 10,000 times by Abba in this way.

Each kiss is precious, by the way. I've never grown complacent or nonchalant about His kisses. They are too powerful to ignore or dismiss lightly. I would never want to despise any of Abba's displays of affection to me, no matter how many times He pours them out.

Will Abba ever stop kissing me daily? I certainly hope not. But beyond that hope, I have assurance that He "does not change."[126] I fully expect to be kissed by Abba every day into eternity in heaven. I don't believe He will stop showering affection on me once I arrive in heaven. The method may change, but the kisses won't stop. This I know for sure:

*Abba is **relentless** with His affection.*

Does Abba "Kiss" *You* Daily?

I'm convinced that He does just that. He shows no partiality (Proverbs 28:21) or favoritism (Acts 10:34; Ephesians 6:9), so if He kisses me

---

126. See James 1:17.

every day, He kisses *you* every day. I believe Abba was kissing me every day *before* 1998 when I finally became aware of something happening daily (my 444 sightings). He may, in fact, have been using a different method all those prior years to kiss me and I didn't see or feel it. I don't know the track record before 1998, but I certainly *do* know it since then.

I want to encourage you to discover Abba's daily kisses in your own life. The kisses can be quite different for different children in His family. I see 444. A friend of mine finds heart-shaped rocks virtually every day and has a large collection of them now. Another friend finds dimes almost every day. Some friends see different repeated numbers. The list goes on. You may hear a special song that just seems to happen by chance on the radio right when you need encouragement. For other folks, a special bird may alight on your windowsill every day. You get the idea.

If you have noticed a pattern of kisses from your Abba, even if they are not yet perceived daily, please start making a record of them and ask Him to sharpen your senses to perceive them more often. If you are not sure if you are noticing kisses from your Abba, then take a few moments to pray, asking Him (with thanksgiving *a la* Philippians 4:6-7) to reveal to you *how* He is kissing you every day. I am convinced you will be blessed if you do so, because your Abba delights in delighting you. He is an affectionate Father; He is the very *best*. If I can jest (in part), Abba *must* kiss you every day because He is a Jewish Father. Mmmwaaah. Here are three summary statements that I believe are true:

*Abba **kisses** His kids every day.*

*Abba loves to **encourage** His kids every day.*

*Abba loves to **affirm** His kids every day.*

The Window of Generations

"Father, why didn't You just make us all at once?"

I asked Abba that strange question just a few years ago, as I was meditating on the restoration of patriarchal leadership in His family today. I was pondering what must have been on God's mind as He began the human race with Adam and wanted him to be fruitful with Eve and fill the earth. It occurred to me that it might have been more efficient, and surely a lot quicker, if God had made all of us right along with Adam and Eve instead.

Because He is able, He could have, of course, made us all at once, yet with distinct personalities and talents, skills, and aptitudes. And surely there was enough dirt to accomplish the task. If I were God (shudder), I would have seriously considered doing the whole job at once and then resting for a while. Why wait for thousands of years for humans to multiply? As they say in Texas, why not just git 'er dun?

Yet, He had apparently decided to have the human race multiply and populate the earth reproductively, beginning with Adam and Eve.[127] Something must have been in His heart that caused Him to decide on this way and not a method something like my proposal. I've learned that Abba is entirely motivated by love. He *is* Love. So, the more fundamental question undergirding my somewhat flippant question above is this:

---

127. See Genesis 1:28.

Windows to the Father's Heart

*"Abba, what aspect of Your incredible love motivated
You to design the population of the earth via
generational reproduction?"*

The answer I received through an impression of joy in my heart from Abba was this revelation: If Abba had made us all at the same time, we would have missed the joy of parenthood. We will pursue this huge (infinite) sector of Abba's heart in the chapter entitled The Window of Joy, but for now let me just summarize by declaring that:[128]

Abba wants to share His joy with you.

Abba was delighted with His son Adam, sharing walks[129] with him in the cool of the day and eagerly anticipating the names that His son would give[130] (or impart) to all the beasts of the field and all the birds of the air. (This recounts just two explicit scriptural records of His activity with Adam.) Surely, Abba anticipated a multitude of other delights because of His relationship with His son, Adam. As we've pointed out before, Abba withholds no good thing from him whose walk is blameless,[131] and this includes the incredible joy of parenthood He wanted to give to Adam (who began as blameless) and, by extension, to all believers (who became blameless through the blood sacrifice of Jesus). In summary,

*Generations exist because of God's love-motivated
sharing of joy.*

There is so very much more, however, that we can explore through The Window of Generations. Let's look at some examples.

Generational Overlap

God's presumed original design for the race called *adam* was, as the Hebrew word implies, for all the generations following Adam

---

128. See Matthew 25:21, 23 and John 15:11 (AMP).
129. Implied by Genesis 3:8-9.
130. See Genesis 2:19-20.
131. See Psalm 84:11.

and Eve to coexist as a *unit* or *organism* or, simply put, one *family* (of God). Death did not enter the picture until Adam and Eve sinned. If they had not done so then it would have been possible, if no succeeding generation sinned either, for all of Adam's descendants to coexist, living harmoniously together upon the earth as it "filled up" with the addition of one generation after another.[132]

Apparently, Abba's desire was for each generation to enjoy the fellowship of the other generations, both previous and successive. Much can be said, of course, about the particulars of this intergenerational blessing and the enjoyment they share, based on only our own limited experience with just three or four coexisting generations today.

But there is something else, another expectation, that was in the heart of Abba that would have been possible if sin had not entered the race called *adam*. Namely, the wisdom, knowledge, and experience gained by previous generations could have been passed down to all the succeeding generations, without loss due to death, and also passed up to the previous generations too. Truly, each generation could have continued forever to share ever-increasing accumulated "treasures" with all the generations before and after their own. There would have been a huge and increasing wealth of knowledge and wisdom that would have been preserved and could be verified (fairly) easily with the living originators if need be. There would possibly have been only limited need for repeated discovery of such treasures in generations subsequent to the original generation of discoverers.

I have no idea how long it will take for a satisfying chunk of the content of the preceding paragraph to sink in for you. I still haven't succeeded in fully mining this revelation myself, nor do I expect that I will ever actually arrive at anything close to a complete understanding. I do expect that in heaven we will be continually learning from all the generations that are there. More on that later.

---

132. It is interesting to speculate on what would have happened to *reproduction* once the earth was filled with universally alive members of Adam's family. Hmm.

The Overlapping Generations of the Patriarchs

Some of the treasures in God's Word are somewhat hidden[133] until we examine the sequences and patterns in more detail. In the present context, let's look at the very long lives of the early patriarchs and how significantly their generations overlapped with each other. I constructed the charts below using information (mostly unambiguous) from the Bible alone,[134] piecing together many bits of lifespan data and the timings of the births and deaths of the patriarchs' sons.

On page 107 is a table of the data used for the charts that follow. Included are the Scriptures that were used to generate the data from biblical information.

From the first four columns of the above table, it is possible to display in graphic form the overlaps of the generations of the early patriarchs (see page 108).

From this bar chart of the patriarchs' life spans, we can glean some interesting information. The lightly shaded bars represent the years spanning the time between Adam's creation and the births of the patriarchs. The dark bars represent the years spanned by the lives of the patriarchs. By simply laying a straight-edge rule vertically on top of this chart at a particular year value (the horizontal axis), one can easily see which patriarchs lived at the same time, or coexisted.

Using this simple method, we can count the number of generations that coexisted with a given patriarch, the number of his prior generations (fathers) that coexisted with him, and also the number of his succeeding generations (sons, grandsons, etc.) that he would have (technically) been able to know (coexist with). These numbers are displayed in separate columns in the table on page 107 and are displayed in the graphic on page 109.

---

133. This may be an *understatement*.

134. For the age of Jacob when Reuben was born, however, we consulted Charles L. Zimmerman, "The Chronology and Birth of Jacob's Children by Leah and her Handmaid," Grace Journal (Winter 1972), volume 13.1, p. 3-12. Because some verses can have different interpretations regarding the immediate succession of father to son, there are a range of other possibilities.

Life Spans of the Patriarchs

Name	Birth Year	Life Span	Death Year	Total Coexiting Generations	Age of Parenthood	# of Former Generations Alive	# of Succeeding Generations Alive	Source(s) for data
Adam	0	930	930	9	130	0	8	Gen 5:4,5
Seth	130	912	1042	9	105	1	7	Gen 5:3,7,8
Enosh	235	905	1140	9	90	2	6	Gen 5:6,10,11
Kenan	325	910	1235	9	70	3	5	Gen 5:9,13,14
Mahalalel	395	895	1290	9	65	4	4	Gen 5:12,16,17
Jared	460	962	1422	9	162	5	3	Gen 5:15,19,20
Enoch	622	365	987	9	55	6	2	Gen 5:18,22,23
Methuselah	687	969	1656	9	187	7	3	Gen 5:21,26,27
Lamech	874	777	1651	9	182	8	2	Gen 5:25,30,31
Noah	1056	950	2006	11	500	6	10	Gen 5:28,32; 9:28,29
Shem	1558	600	2158	11	100	3	9	Gen 7:11; 11:2,11
Arphaxad	1658	438	2096	11	35	2	8	Gen 11:10,12,13
Shelah	1693	433	2126	11	30	3	7	Gen 11:12,14,15
Eber	1723	464	2187	11	34	4	6	Gen 11:14,16,17
Peleg	1757	239	1996	11	30	5	5	Gen 11:16,18,19
Reu	1787	239	2026	11	32	6	4	Gen 11:18,20,21
Serug	1819	230	2049	11	30	7	3	Gen 11:20,22,23
Nahor	1849	148	1997	11	29	8	2	Gen 11:22,24,25
Terah	1878	205	2083	11	70	9	2	Gen 11:24,32
Abram	1948	175	2113	11	85	10	2	Gen 11:26; 17:24,26; 25:7; *
Isaac	2048	180	2228	8	60	7	2	Gen 21:5; 35:28
Jacob	2108	147	2255	6	84	5	2	Gen 25:26; 47:28; **
Joseph	2198	110	2292	6		2	2	Gen 50:22,26

* 85 = Age of Abraham when Ishmael was born
** 84 = Age of Jacob when Reuben was born

107

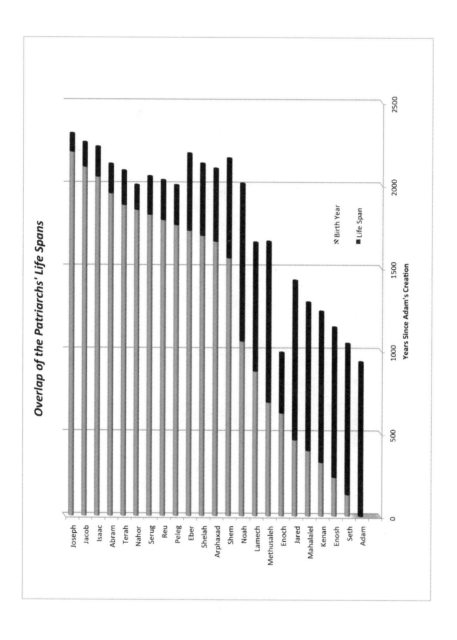

Overlap of the Patriarchs' Life Spans

The Window of Generations

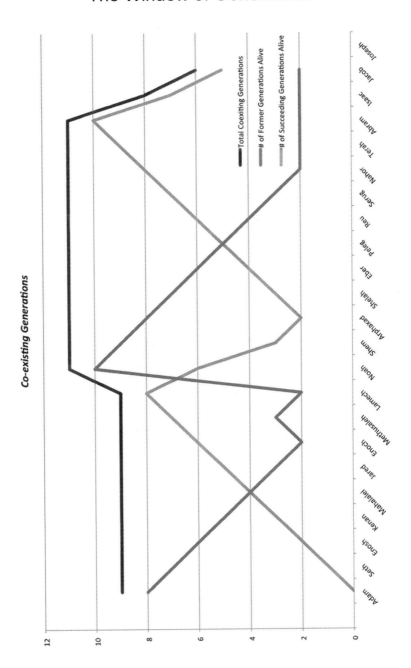

109

Windows to the Father's Heart

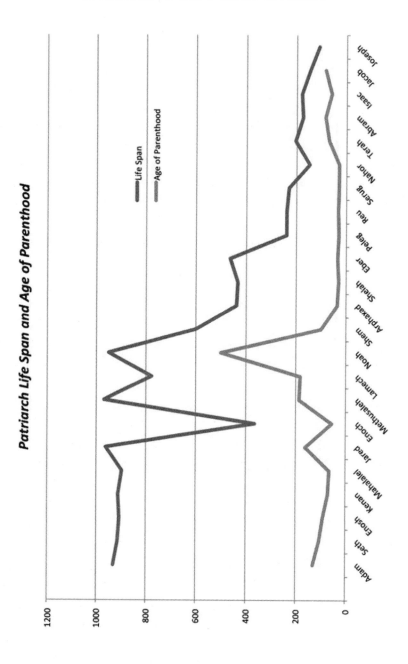

Patriarch Life Span and Age of Parenthood

Life Span
Age of Parenthood

Adam, Seth, Enosh, Kenan, Mahalalel, Jared, Enoch, Methuselah, Lamech, Noah, Shem, Arphaxad, Shelah, Eber, Peleg, Reu, Serug, Nahor, Terah, Abram, Isaac, Jacob, Joseph

The Window of Generations

The top line in the graph shows the number of generations that coexisted with each of the patriarchs. It is very interesting to note that it was exactly nine for many generations and then increased to exactly eleven for Noah all the way down to Abram. Only then did the number of coexisting generations decrease and eventually settle at three or four by modern times. This graphic alone confirms the loving desire of Abba to see His family blessed with several generations of fathers and sons living at the same time. The blessing of overlap of several generations was evidently part of the perfect and pleasing will of the Father. Even though the sin of Adam and Eve prevented all the generations from coexisting, Abba nevertheless still arranged for nine to eleven of them to have that simultaneous blessing, all the way to Abram. There is a clear conclusion:

Abba loves to see the generations blessed through coexistence.

It is very exciting to think about the restoration of this manifestation of Abba's love that all believers will experience one day in heaven, because then all the generations of saints will be reunited forever. What a great time that will be!

Of further interest is the *manner* in which the total number of coexisting generations remained high for so long. The number of former generations (fathers) that coexisted with a given patriarch increased after Adam, of course, as the number of successive generations increased while the fathers were still alive. But the number of generations of descendants (sons) of a given patriarch decreased and the net result is a constant number (nine) of coexisting generations until the time of Noah. This is significant and leads to an astounding conclusion as we shall see.

For Noah and the succeeding patriarchs down to Abram, the number of coexisting generations is higher (eleven) and constant, but for a different reason. The number of generations of succeeding sons increases rapidly as the age of parenthood drops precipitously after Noah. (This is illustrated in the graph on page 110, where the top curve represents life span and the bottom curve represents the age at which a given patriarch is recorded as having his first son.) In other words the appearance of successive generations accelerated dramatically, even as the life spans of the patriarchs after Noah began to drop extremely rapidly with successive generations. The net result is *still* a large number of coexisting generations (eleven).

This was only possible because Noah did not have sons until he was 500 years old, and those successive sons began to have their own children at the ages of between 29 and 35 until Terah slowed down. Evidently, it was Abba's desire to help Noah obey His command[135] to be fruitful and multiply, similar to the command[136] given to Adam, but now with the apparent motive to still bless the family with a large number of coexisting generations. Another outcome of this phenomenon was of course a much-accelerated increase in population growth after the flood.

It is important to point out that the number of coexisting generations for a given patriarch is the maximum number reached *at some time in his life*. It is not the case that each patriarch had the blessing of *always* having a large number of generations coexisting with him *throughout* his lifetime. For Noah the fluctuation is dramatic: there were six generations of his fathers alive at his birth, one generation of sons at the time of the flood, and ultimately he "saw" ten generations of his descendants by the time he died at the age of 950.

Abba Showed Mercy to All the Fathers of Noah

There is yet another profound discovery awaiting the hunter of Abba's love for fathers when we ask the question: Why did Noah have sons only after the age of 500? One possible answer occurred to me as I pondered this question while staring at the Age of Parenthood graph for a while. Noah stands out remarkably in this graph. The longest any other patriarch "had to wait" before having children was only 187 years (Noah's grandfather, Methusaleh), and the next longest wait (182 years) was experienced by Noah's father, Lamech. Noah's wait of 500 years before having sons surpasses the waits of his father and grandfather by

---

135. See Genesis 9:1.

136. See Genesis 1:28.

The Window of Generations

more than 310 years. No one else even comes close to Noah's record of parental delay, before or since.

Why did Abba make Noah wait that long? He wasn't being mean. The answer to this question is a profound one. The clue lies in the fact that all of Noah's fathers (the generations before him) had died by the time of the flood when Noah was 600 years old. His grandfather, Methusaleh, died in the year of the flood,[137] and his father, Lamech, six years before that. None of the fathers of Noah were still alive at the time of the flood.

Here is a possible explanation: because Abba was clearly in charge of when the flood occurred, I believe that He arranged the timing of the flood and the life spans of Noah's fathers so that none of Noah's direct line of fathers before him had to witness the horror of watching all their progeny (excepting Noah and his sons and their wives) perish. Perhaps they would have been allotted seats on the ark if they had still been alive, but none of their other family lines beside Noah's were destined for survival.

I believe that Abba so honored the holiness of Noah's fatherly line (including Lamech and Methusaleh) that He spared them the horror of watching their other sons and daughters[138] and families wiped out. In other words, Abba showed mercy to all the fathers of Noah. Abba, having the progenitor Father-heart, could not bear to allow Noah's fathers to witness the tragedy that was coming. He had compassion and understanding of how they would feel and was careful to protect their hearts from such horrific pain.

Abba spared Noah's fathers the horror of watching their other descendants perish.

Perhaps one reason why Noah did not have sons until he was 500 years old was so that the flood could be timed for the year when the last of Noah's fathers had passed away and Noah did not yet have a big family.

---

137. See Genesis 5:25-29; 7:11. With this information, one can calculate that Methusaleh died in the year of the flood.

138. See Genesis 5:26, 30.

113

These two conditions constrained Noah to have his children much, much later in life. There was, however, a resulting paucity of generations coexisting with Noah right before the flood. Perhaps Abba arranged for accelerated generational growth of Noah's family after the flood in order to bless him with significant generational overlap in his later years.[139]

How many progeny did Noah likely have by the time he died? We can estimate this number by looking far forward to the descendants of Jacob during their 400 years of captivity in Egypt. Even though it is not clear what the average age of parenthood was during this time period, we do know that it would be roughly similar to that during the time of Noah, if not longer.[140] During those 400 years, the number of Israelites had increased to approximately 2 million men, with probably the same approximate number of women, plus children. Comparing this to the 70 or so in Jacob's family who emigrated to Egypt from the land of Canaan during the famine, we see an example of how, over the course of say ten generations, a small group of Israelites grew to millions. Thus, it is likely that Noah's progeny numbered at least in the hundreds of thousands during the 350 years after his sons started having children (just after the flood ended), with at least nine generations having appeared during that time.[141]

Restoration of Generational Coexistence in Heaven

This window into the heart of Abba concerning generational coexistence gives us an appreciation for the blessing that is to come one day in heaven, as all our (saved) ancestors we will find there, along with all our believing progeny, will live with us forever, together. It is thrilling to speculate on what that blessing will entail, but at the very least we can surely believe that the original intent of Abba for the fullness of family joy will be realized.

---

139. Noah lived another 350 years after the flood.

140. The average age of parenthood had increased again to about seventy during the generations of Terah down to Jacob. See chart above.

141. You can easily imagine that if Noah had started having children at say, the age of 200, then the number of arks necessary to contain his whole family 400 years later would have been a fleet so large it would be the envy of modern day admirals.

The Window of Curiosity

"Father, why...?"

One of my earliest memories from my young boyhood was an experience one night that impacted the rest of my life.

Our family often traveled by car between Eugene, Oregon (where I was born and lived until the age of eight) and Portland, where my paternal grandparents lived. Even though the drive required only about two hours, to my four-year-old mind it seemed to be *really* long and prompted the proverbial, and frequent, question to my dad, the driver: "Daddy, are we there yet?" He always patiently replied, "We'll be there soon, son." Needless to say, I had trouble with understanding the meaning of "soon," often leading to the same question to Dad ten minutes later.

On one of those trips northward on the open highway during the nighttime, the cloudless sky was filled with zillions of stars and a big full moon just above the eastern horizon. I remember being captivated by the view through my backseat side window[142] as I watched the moon in particular doing something that I thought was really weird. As we zoomed past one tall Douglas fir tree after another on the roadside, the moon seemed to me to be "following" us on the other side of trees. It looked to my young mind like it was flying along at the same speed as

---

142. That may have been the first time I was treated to a cloudless view of the stars and full moon near the horizon on such a drive in the normally rainy environment of the Pacific Northwest.

our car, because it held the same position outside my window for a *long* time (probably one of my ten-minute "eternities").

I was captivated by the moon's behavior and asked my dad,

"Daddy, why is the moon following us?"

I'm sure my dad must have struggled a bit in trying to explain this "creepy" moon behavior, as he gave an adult answer that puzzled me: "Because it is so far away, son, it just looks like it is following us." I didn't get it. I was still mystified, and still thought it was following us. But I remember thinking, "I want to know why it is following us, even though Daddy says it just looks like it."[143]

So, I became a physicist.

That is, I began to ask the question, "Why?" in many arenas of delightful discovery concerning God's wondrous creation and how it works. I was so intensely curious about the "why" and "how" of nature that I woke up one morning with a Ph.D. in physics.

Curiosity is a thread running through several of the perspectives that have been looking into the Father's heart through several windows in this book.[144] Let's explore a little deeper into that infinite heart by asking,

"Why do we ask, 'Why?'"

In other words, what motivated Abba to give us curiosity? This is a deep question, and has several levels at which we might search for answers. However, let's focus on Abba's amazing desire, founded on His infinite love for us, to cause our very souls to long for knowledge of Him and His creation. Another way to phrase this question is to ask, "Why didn't Abba just *impute* to us all the knowledge He wanted us to have? Why do we have to learn it?"

---

143. This may well have been my first experience with the confusion that can occur because of the difference between perception and reality.

144. As described in the Introduction, even this book is a result of my desire to "see" more and more of my Abba's heart.

The Window of Curiosity

We know that curiosity is a trait that does not have to be learned. Anyone can see it manifested in the behavior of even a newborn infant as his or her eyes roam everywhere. Some of that behavior may be instinctual, of course, and shared by many species of animals, but there are many examples that parents can point to when their children began to explore their surroundings simply because they were seemingly curious.

Some may answer that we are curious because we are made in the image of a curious God, although others might counter that an omniscient God couldn't possibly be curious. My personal belief is that Abba delights Himself in delaying His awareness of some of our decisions,[145] so that He experiences the pleasure of our good choices.[146] Given that the curiosity of God is a debatable matter, and thus may occupy your meditations for a considerable length of time, let's instead remember another theme for the motivations of Abba, one which we have already pointed out a few times:

*Abba is blessed when **you** are blessed.*

This begs the question of whether curiosity is a blessing or perhaps a curse? As we shall see, the answer depends, as in many other areas of life, on the choices made.

The Agony and the Ecstasy of Perpetual Curiosity

When I was still a professor at the University of Southern California (USC) and a relatively new Christian, two representatives from the honor students' campus group, The Mortar Board Society, paid a visit to my office. They extended a very gracious invitation to present a "last lecture" in the annual series of lectures by that name. Faculty lecturers were asked to pretend that they were giving their "last lecture," which motivated them to consider their overriding passion and/or most important topic with which, "for the last time," to stimulate the thinking

---

145. For example, Abba desired to see what His son, Adam, would choose to name all the creatures brought before him (Genesis 2:19).

146. See the discussion in the chapter entitled The Window of Choice.

of the student audience. I remember marveling at the brilliance of that challenge.

I was honored by their invitation and further honored when they informed me that the lecture series had been dormant for twenty years, and they wanted *me* to re-inaugurate the Last Lectures at USC. No pressure. When I considered how much time and effort it would take to prepare a truly outstanding lecture to a broad audience of extremely gifted students, I realized that this endeavor might just require more hours than I could squeeze out of my already packed schedule. I politely thanked them for graciously honoring me and declined the invitation.

They didn't give up easily, however, and asked me to please give it some more thought over the coming week and then make a decision. Right then I knew that this suggestion was not from them but from the Holy Spirit, whom I felt was actually prompting me to *pray* about the invitation. So I did, and after only one day I became convinced that I was being encouraged by Abba to give a powerful message about *Him*. The honor students had extended the offer to speak on *any* subject I wished, with no restraints or controls.

But I still didn't know what topic I could possibly talk about that would satisfy the students' hunger for thought-provoking material and, at the same time, convey a message about God to a primarily secular audience. Indeed, the audience would include faculty advisors (most if not all of whom would be atheists or agnostics) who would rapidly become cross-armed, scowling critics if I spoke on a Christian theme. I made a "deal" with the Holy Spirit: "If You will give me the title of the Last Lecture You want me to deliver, then I will do it."

That offer drew a loud chuckle from the Holy Spirit, and instantly the following title popped into my spirit: "The Agony and the Ecstasy of Perpetual Curiosity." Wow, what a bizarre title. The Holy Spirit had kept His part of my proposed bargain, so now I needed to keep my part. But He did much *more* than that. Over the next twenty minutes, I sketched some thoughts on my notepad (the old-fashioned kind made out of trees), and I realized I was done preparing the lecture. Not only was I given the title, but also three main talking points that would fit into about thirty to forty minutes, leaving time for some discussion afterward.

I called the student representatives and accepted their invitation. I had the lecture ready to go. What a wonderful example of the "elephant-mouse" partnership.[147] All I had to do was what I had agreed to do—deliver the lecture. I must say that I had tremendous joy and anticipation as the lecture day approached. I knew that a foundational decision was going to be placed before these students who were especially gifted intellectually. When the lecture commenced, I was filled to overflowing with the Holy Spirit. Here are the three main, inspired points of the lecture, according to different levels (or arenas) of contrast (agony vs. ecstasy) in connection with our curiosity. In them, you will see a progression "into" Abba's heart.

A Scientist *Never* Knows If He Is Right, Only If He Is Wrong

The scientific method for advancement of knowledge is inherently masochistic. Here's why: the scientific method basically consists of the following steps or stages:

(1) Putting forward a *hypothesis* (a fancy word for "guess") that is based on the observed facts up to that time and is *capable of being tested* in the laboratory or through future observation. Creative ideas "popping into" brains, "flashes" of insight, "light bulbs going on," as well as "aha" moments are all ways of describing the genius aspect of this essential step that can catapult advancement of knowledge and understanding through the proposal of the hypothesis.

(2) Developing the logical consequences of the hypothesis, such as "explaining" previous mysteries, but also including the (ideally) objective guidance of the researcher in suggesting ways to *test* the predictions that can be deduced from the hypothesis. In other words, how would someone be able to prove that it (the hypothesis)

---

147. See the chapter entitled The Window of Support.

is wrong or incomplete? This step is where the inherent masochism starts to manifest.

(3) Experimental testing of the predictions based on the hypothesis, preferably by more than one researcher or one research group. A useful ("successful") hypothesis "makes sense" out of previous mysteries or confusion and advances the horizons of understanding in a particular arena of investigation. In addition, the testing should ideally probe deeply enough into the "unknown" arenas to discover where the hypothesis meets its own limitation of applicability or even indictment of its basic premise(s). In other words, finding out how the hypothesis is "wrong" or "incomplete."

(4) Based on the discovered "failures" of the hypothesis (in step 3), identifying possible improvements, new directions of thought, extensions of the hypothesis, etc. to try to enhance the power or effectiveness of the hypothesis in such a way that this new, improved hypothesis can serve as a new starting point (step 1) of the method.

Here is the sobering conclusion regarding the emotional effect of the scientific method though: The scientist can never know if he or she is *right* but only how he or she is *wrong*! No matter how extensively the hypothesis seems to stand up under detailed scrutiny, there is always the possibility that it will somehow fail or prove to be incomplete upon further, or deeper, investigation. The scientific method is inherently a method of *negation* and fundamentally limited in its *affirmative* power.

This is the *agony* that awaits the scientist in every pursuit of knowledge through the scientific method. It is only a matter of time until he or she is proven *wrong* in some manner. On the positive side, there is the *ecstasy* (the thrill) of discovery of a new concept or manner of understanding that seems to remove some mysteries and open up new vistas of thinking about the subject at hand. Sometimes, there is a huge *revolutionary* idea that truly changes the paradigm for a particular field of investigation. This is what a scientist *lives* for.

In summary, for the scientist there is a clear contrast that stems from his or her curiosity:

The Window of Curiosity

Agony: ***never*** *knowing if you are right*

Ecstasy: the thrill of discovery of new or novel approaches or insights

Moral Implications of Curiosity

There is another level or arena of contrast that stems from this curiosity that leads to discovery. This is particularly evident with technologies that are birthed through the satisfaction of curiosity of one or maybe thousands of knowledge seekers. Many technological discoveries are essentially amoral, meaning that they are not right or wrong but simply morally neutral.

What constitutes right or wrong is often viewed as a matter of opinion (moral relativism) but can sometimes be illuminated through objective or absolute moral measures (e.g., a moral code that is established from a higher or external source). Leaving aside that issue for the moment, let's look at two familiar examples that give insight into the tension between the agony and ecstasy of curiosity.

The discoveries that enabled the development of sustained nuclear fission reactions can (and have been) used for the production of (sometimes safe) energy to help enhance the lifestyle of many millions of people. On the other hand, the same basic discoveries were ultimately used to develop explosive chain reactions (fission weapons[148]) that were used on Hiroshima and Nagasaki in 1945 to end World War II. There are pros and cons to both of these uses, and what those are varies with the opinions of different individuals.

Nevertheless, from the point of view of the discoverers and developers of these different uses, there is often an emotionally disturbing (or agonizing) realization of the harm that can come from the original curiosity, though it is the case that the amount or level of agony might be drastically different (or non-existent) for different coworkers involved with the same project. This was true for the Manhattan Project

---

148. These are often mistakenly referred to as atomic bombs, when in fact they are nuclear bombs.

that led to the first fission bombs used to end World War II. Usually the ecstasy of discovery precedes the sobering agony of such discovery, but sometimes the ecstasy is amplified by tremendously exciting beneficial uses of the technology only evident years later.

The point being made here is that curiosity can lead, along the morality avenue, to agony on one hand through horrific use of the fruit of curiosity or to ecstasy, on the other hand, through wonderful and beneficial use of the same fruit. The appearance of agony or ecstasy depends on the choices made regarding the use of the fruit of curiosity.

Another example in this regard is particularly stark—a hammer and nails can be used to build a house or to nail someone to a cross. The hammer and nails are morally neutral, but the morality contrast of these two choices in their use is quite distinct by almost anyone's standards.

It should be pointed out that the curiosity-motivated discoverers of hammers and nails most likely had no idea that one day they would be used to nail Jesus (or anyone) to a cross. Similar considerations apply to the discoverers of human-initiated nuclear fission. Yet, in the hands of the collective population, there was an evolution in the use of these tools along very different lines than those originally intended. Thus, we can see that the curiosity given to us by Abba can either result in agony or in ecstasy, depending on our choices.

Curiosity Forever?

There is a much more important arena, however, than the two we have already (very briefly) introduced. Let me pose the following question:

Does Abba take away our curiosity when we arrive in heaven?

Our answer may depend on how we view His love toward us. On the one hand, we could surmise that everything will become clear upon our arrival in heaven because we won't be fumbling around with our clumsy investigative methods but shall lovingly receive truth directly from the Holy Spirit. There is merit to that view, of course, because it was promised by Jesus that the Holy Spirit would guide us into all truth,[149] and of course He has been doing that already.

On the other hand, we already peered through The Window of Eternity to discover that Abba's revelation of His love for us will require an infinite time because that love is itself infinite. There may be other aspects of His nature that will be revealed progressively as well, so this view also has our attention, to say the least. I personally believe that both viewpoints will have (and do have) application, with some knowledge revealed in a heartbeat, while other knowledge (an infinite amount) will necessarily be progressively revealed to us as we explore Abba's heart forever.

There are at least two facets of our nature, given to us by Abba, that I believe will never cease—creativity[150] and curiosity. If you accept the belief that we were created with curiosity by Abba, and that we were created to live forever with that curiosity as part of our nature, then a very important decision comes to the forefront and stares us directly in our face. Namely, we need to choose the environment in which we will be curious forever.

Everyone needs to realize that they will live forever. Abba made eternity, and us to live eternally, because of His infinite love for us. The problem is that we have free will and can choose to live *apart* from Abba forever because of our denial of His offer of eternal life[151] or to live forever *with* Him in eternal, blissful relationship.

If you choose the former then you will still exist forever, but in an environment that is totally devoid of the truth and where there are no trustworthy answers to your questions, born of curiosity. In other words, your curiosity will never be satisfied, and a certain and eternal agony awaits you. If you desire truth in your innermost being, that would be sheer agony, as you would have no hope of ever having reliable answers to your questions again.

---

149. See John 16:13.

150. This is explored in the chapter entitled Window of Creativity.

151. See John 3:16.

If however, you *do* accept Abba's offer of eternal life *with* Him in Paradise, then you will *always* find, or receive, answers to your "Why?" questions. In heaven, you *can* know if you are right, because the Spirit of Truth will be revealing *absolute* truth to you, guiding you as you exercise your still-existent free will to follow your curiosity along exquisite pathways of discovery. This proverb will still apply:

> *It is the glory of God to conceal a matter; to search*
> *out a matter is the glory of kings* (Proverbs 25:2).

Most readers of this book will have already made their choice. But, if you haven't yet done so, please consider your only two options as totally distinct consequences of your perpetual curiosity:

(1) Incredible, delightful ecstasy in *always* finding more absolute truth, with no "maybes." Your curiosity will always be an amazing blessing forever.

Or:

(2) Horrible isolation in darkness, *never* finding reliable answers to satisfy your eternal hunger to know. Your curiosity will become a terrible curse.

The choice is *yours*.

The Window of Turning

"Father, why did You choose Elijah to turn our hearts?"

Abba wants fathers and children to be in godly relationship, so much so that He is intent on *doing something* about it. You may recall this powerful promise He made through His prophet, Malachi:

> *Behold, I am going to send you Elijah the prophet before the coming of the great and terrible day of the Lord. He will turn the hearts of the fathers to their children, and the hearts of the children to their fathers [a reconciliation produced by repentance], so that I will not come and strike the land with a curse [of complete destruction]* (Malachi 4:5-6 AMP).

There is much to be mined from this passage, of course, but I want to focus on a question that I had just a few years ago, after having read this promise many times:

> *"Abba, why did You choose Elijah to turn our hearts?"*

Why not Abraham, for example? After all, he is called Father Abraham, not only by the Jewish people, but also by all Gentile believers who have since been "grafted in" to his family.[152] There is no scriptural record of Elijah ever having any natural children. So, why would he "qualify" to be the agent of turning generational hearts back to each other? One possibility is that he might somehow be encouragement to

---

152. See Romans 11:11-24.

those who are also without natural children, as he *did* have a spiritual son, Elisha, who called him father.[153] But it seemed to me that there must be a deeper reason why Abba chose to send Elijah rather than anyone else.

Another possible reason is due to the fact that Elijah never died but was taken up in a whirlwind.[154] Perhaps he was "available" to be sent again to the earth? Here again, by itself this seems to be an inadequate qualification because Elijah's next recorded appearance (on the Mount of Transfiguration[155]) was also accompanied by Moses (who did die[156]) when they both visited Jesus and His three "closest" disciples (Peter, James, and John). Furthermore, Enoch was also "taken,"[157] and in fact was a forefather of Abraham and therefore might be regarded as more qualified than Elijah. So, not physically dying could not be the sole reason for Abba's choice of Elijah.

As I kept asking Abba, "Why Elijah?" there finally was some guidance for me by the Holy Spirit. And it was based on a particular verse in a scriptural account I had read many times—namely, the confrontation by Elijah with the prophets of Baal on Mount Carmel.[158] Elijah had challenged these prophets to a contest to see whose god was the real God—Baal or the God of Abraham, Isaac, and Israel. The god who was able to send fire upon a sacrifice offered to Him would be demonstrated as the real God. The prophets of Baal failed miserably as they tried to demonstrate the reality of their god through their various entreaties for him to send fire.

When it was Elijah's turn, he rebuilt the altar to God that was there, prepared the sacrifice of a bull by cutting it into pieces and laying them on the wood he had placed on the altar, and then he took the

---

153. See 2 Kings 2:12.

154. See 2 Kings 2:1-11.

155. See Matthew 17:1-8; Mark 9:2-8; Luke 9:28-36.

156. See Joshua 1:2.

157. See Genesis 5:24.

158. See 1 Kings 18:16-45.

unusual step of dousing the sacrifice completely with water.[159] For fire to now consume the sacrifice, there must clearly be a manifestation of supernatural power. That is exactly what happened when Elijah called on God to send fire on his sacrifice, and the prophets of Baal were not only humiliated by losing the contest, they were also killed according to the subsequent order by Elijah.[160]

The "Prophet of Turning"

Let me focus now on the particular plea that Elijah made to God before the consuming fire came:

> *At the time of sacrifice, the prophet Elijah stepped forward and prayed: "Lord, the God of Abraham, Isaac and Israel, let it be known today that you are God in Israel and that I am your servant and have done all these things at your command. Answer me, O Lord, answer me, so these people will know that you, O Lord, are God, and that you are **turning their hearts back again**"* (1 Kings 18:35-37).

Elijah recognized that God was turning the hearts of the Israelites back to Him again, and it seemed to matter greatly to him that God was doing so. Elijah's heart was so tuned to the desire in God's heart that His people turn back to Him that God marked Elijah that very day (if not before) as his Prophet of Turning. Because of Elijah's sensitivity to, and sharing in, this passion in God's heart for such a turning at that point in Israel's history, I believe he became the choice of God as His agent for the heart-turning in the distant future[161] spoken of over four centuries later by Malachi.

And Elijah *did* come, about nine centuries after his first ministry on the earth. As the "inner circle" of disciples (Peter, James, and John) came down the Mount of Transfiguration with Jesus, they were instructed not

---

159. It may be of interest to note that this dousing of the sacrifice with water was done *three times* with four large jars of water. This is one of the 4-4-4 occurrences in Scripture that I researched in connection with the mystery described in The Window of Affection.

160. See 1 Kings 18:40.

161. Namely, at the time of John the Baptist and beyond.

to tell anyone what they had seen (the appearance of Moses and Elijah and Jesus' transfiguration) until Jesus had risen from the dead.[162] This apparently caused them some confusion concerning the timing of the "great and terrible day of the Lord" referred to by their teachers (who were presumably quoting Malachi), who had told them that Elijah must come first. So they discussed[163] what Jesus meant by "rising from the dead." Perhaps they were wondering if Jesus meant that He would "rise" *before* Elijah came? Jesus made it clear that Elijah had already come:

> *Jesus replied, "To be sure, Elijah comes and will restore all things. But I tell you, Elijah has already come, and they did not recognize him, but have done to him everything they wished. In the same way the Son of Man is going to suffer at their hands." Then the disciples understood that he was talking to them about John the Baptist* (Matthew 17:11-13).

Elijah had already appeared as an "agent" or "influencer" operating through (or upon) John the Baptist to preach repentance (heart-turning). After John the Baptist was beheaded, Elijah appeared again (with Moses) to Jesus and the three disciples on the Mount of Transfiguration. This begs the question: "Is Elijah still operating today to turn the hearts of fathers to their children and vice versa?" I believe the answer is "yes," and much more. Jesus promised in Matthew 17:11 that Elijah would restore "all things."[164] This broadens the mandate of Elijah considerably. One of the related "things" being restored, in my opinion, is the original design of leadership for God's family.

The Restoration of Patriarchal Leadership

The turning of hearts of fathers to children and of children to their fathers is just one aspect of the broader restoration of "all things" by Elijah that Jesus prophesied to the disciples. It is a necessary condition

---

162. See Matthew 17:9.

163. See Mark 9:10.

164. Or, "set things right" (AMP), or "put everything in order" (TPT).

for the reestablishment of Abba's design for the nature of leadership of Adam's family. *Before* there were apostles (or even prophets), the leadership of this family was upon the shoulders of the *fathers* or *patriarchs.*

As we gaze into the Father's heart though The Window of Turning, we can see His desire to reestablish the divine order of patriarchal leadership among the generations. As I reflected on this possibility for several months in 2012, I finally asked Abba the "point-blank" question,

"Abba, are You restoring patriarchal leadership to Your family?"

He answered me with a question (so typical of Him): "Son, if Adam had not sinned, to whom would you be 'answering'[165] today?" I thought for just a moment and answered, "That's easy, Dad, I would be answering to Adam, and all of my fathers between him and me, because they would still be alive." A flood of revelation poured over me as I realized Abba's heart's desire to see the generations restored in relationship.[166]

I can't resist sharing a prophetic blessing that occurred when my grandson Sire was born in October of 2012, and I learned of his name from my daughter and son-in-love. I had not shared my exploration of the restoration of patriarchal leadership prior to Sire's birth, and his parents had not shared their choice of his name with me. When I learned that his given name was Sire, I was blessed tremendously. "Sire" means "king" or "father." My grandson is destined to be a "father-king." I had received a wonderful affirmation of my belief that Abba is restoring patriarchal leadership.

Abba's original design was to have all our fathers "speaking into our lives" as we live on into eternity with each other. Eventually in heaven we will be reunited with *all* of our fathers (and mothers, and children) who are saved, and Abba's original plan will proceed accordingly. What an exciting prospect! Imagine the blessing of patriarchal leadership as our fathers (parents in general) continue to teach and nurture and share

---

165. In the sense of "accountable" or "submitted."

166. See also the discussion in the chapter entitled The Window of Generations.

insights and wisdom with us on into eternity. They will undoubtedly benefit from us as well, because our relationships are two-way in nature.

The progressive generational turning of hearts is not simply a process of making forgiveness for one another a priority, although that may be an essential ingredient. It is also much more than reestablishment of a lifestyle that honors the generations and is committed to esteeming one another. Furthermore, it is not just a delightful discovery of many ways in which to bless one another. All of these aspects, and many others, are fruit of something much deeper and significant that reflects intense desire in the heart of Abba for us all—unity.

Unity

While Abba's reasons for desiring unity in His family are likely to be progressively revealed for eternity, we can be assured that unity is not just a goal to be able to live peaceably with one another. Peaceful coexistence in itself was not an issue until Adam and Eve sinned and will ultimately be restored because of the second Adam's sacrifice. True unity is not a *tool* for accomplishment of projects or goals (such as peace or service), but rather it is a *fruit* of our love for one another.

There is much more in the heart of Abba regarding heart-turning that we can only touch on here, but the knitting of our hearts to each other, and to *His*, serves as a springboard to incredible mutual blessing as our heart-turning begins to yield *the fruit of unity* that lasts. Not just the manifestation of peace, but incredible cooperative creativity[167] will result from this unity. Heart-turning will result in the *knitting* of hearts and expressions of love that will be beyond description.

The Love Transition

One of the possible outcomes is a collective, cooperative phenomenon that has many precedents in the natural world in which a large collection of objects (such as atoms or molecules) can exhibit dramatic shifts (or transitions) in appearance and/or behavior. Examples are the condensation of water vapor into raindrops or the ultra-low-temperature

---

167. See the chapter entitled The Window of Creativity.

phenomenon of superconductivity. There are many other examples that are commonly the purview of physicists and other scientists.

I shared a message[168] in 2009 in which I speculated on the possibility of a love transition occurring among the sons of God that is marked by the perfect unity for which Jesus prayed.[169] The fuel or causative agent for this transition is the increasingly dominant exchange of attractive love among the hearts of the sons of God as they allow themselves to be quieted by the love of Abba.[170] Another possible outcome of such a transition is a bride for Jesus who is perfect, without spot, wrinkle, or blemish.[171] Many other significant and observable outcomes of such a transition will be described in a future writing.

The possible manifestations of blessings arising from our hearts being turned by Elijah toward other generations (previous and subsequent) are thrilling to contemplate. The multi-faceted corporate nature of the body of Christ is magnificent in its designed diversity, purpose on earth, and destiny in heaven.

168. "The Love Transition," delivered at HRock Church, Pasadena, CA, 2009. A written version of this teaching is currently in preparation.

169. See John 17:20-23.

170. See Zephaniah 3:17.

171. See Ephesians 5:27.

The Window of Creativity

"Father, how many of my creations can You fit on Your fridge?"

There is very little (if any) disagreement among the sons of God with the claim that Adam's family is amazingly creative. We don't have to look very far to find evidence of this aspect of our nature that Abba delightfully purposed to give us, beginning with Adam himself:

> Now the Lord God had formed out of the ground all the wild animals and all the birds in the sky. He brought them to the man to see what he would name them; and whatever the man called each living creature, that was its name. So the man gave names to all the livestock, the birds in the sky and all the wild animals (Genesis 2:19-20).

If Abba's anticipation of Adam's creativity in naming the creatures is an indication, then not only did Abba craft creativity in us, but He "looks forward"[172] to see how it will manifest.

The gift of creativity that Abba built into our DNA is one of the most remarkable of all. Combined with the incredible intelligence that Adam exhibited (shown in naming all the creatures), which is being

---

172. As we have indicated elsewhere in this book, this begs the question of whether Abba "limits" His own knowledge in certain situations so that He might presumably be (hopefully pleasantly) "surprised" by our decisions. In the present context, our free will and the decisions that arise from its exercise in the crafting of our creations can somehow cause Abba to "yearn to see" what we will do with this gift.

restored[173] to the people of God because of the work of Jesus on our behalf, our God-given creativity provides avenues for amazing displays of the handiwork of Abba's sons that ultimately bring glory back to Him. There is no limit to what can be accomplished with the gifts Abba has given us:

Everything is possible for one who believes (Mark 9:23).

In a very real sense, we are "extensions" of God's creativity. We are not equal to God, but we are created in His image and likeness[174] and are becoming like Christ;[175] we *resemble* our Abba (the Creator). He derives great joy from His creation, and because His joy in creating is a good thing He is "compelled" to share it with us; in other words, He will not withhold creativity from us.[176] Abba's love-motivated sharing of good things with us is a fantastic blessing that we did not earn or deserve. It was bestowed upon Adam's family simply because it is in our Father's nature is to give freely and not hold anything back (permanently) that is good.

There are, of course, many beneficial outcomes of our creativity, including breakthroughs in medicine and technology to mention just two. A great many proposals for creative (or breakthrough) projects include justifications based on the "good" that will come to mankind as a result of successful completion. But Abba does not need us to justify ourselves when we have creative desire in our hearts. He gave us the gift of creativity *before* our imaginations were encouraged by Him to dream and dream hugely. He delights Himself in us[177] and has immeasurable joy when we receive joy from creating a masterpiece or even from absentmindedly doodling on a piece of paper while chatting on the phone.

---

173. For examples of this promise, see Acts 3:21 and Matthew 17:11.

174. See Genesis 1:26-27.

175. See Romans 8:29.

176. See discussion in the chapter entitled The Window of Eternity, in connection with the promise contained in Psalms 84:11.

177. See Zephaniah 3:17.

The Window of Creativity

Motivation for the Masterpiece?

It is important, however, to identify the motivation for our masterpieces. In a similar consideration to that which we discussed in the chapter entitled The Window of Curiosity, the gift of creativity can result in morally neutral creations but is also capable of producing either harmful or beneficial creations, depending on the motivation of the person(s) who have exercised their creativity. One clear example from Scripture is the building of the Tower of Babel by the pagan men on the plain of Shinar (Babylon) described in Genesis 11:

> *Now the whole world had one language and a common speech. As men moved eastward, they found a plain in Shinar and settled there. They said to each other, "Come, let's make bricks and bake them thoroughly." They used brick instead of stone, and tar for mortar. Then they said, "Come, let us build ourselves a city, with a tower that reaches to the heavens, so that we may make a name for ourselves; otherwise we will be scattered over the face of the whole earth." But the Lord came down to see the city and the tower the people were building. The Lord said, "If as one people speaking the same language they have begun to do this, then nothing they plan to do will be impossible for them. Come, let us go down and confuse their language so they will not understand each other." So the Lord scattered them from there over all the earth, and they stopped building the city* (Genesis 11:1-8).

There are many lessons[178] in this passage, but we can see that the "masterpiece" they created was not pleasing at all to the Lord and was motivated by at least two wicked desires—pride ("a name for ourselves") and self-preservation of power and security (prevention of scattering).

---

178. For example, these pagan men may have "seen" prophetically into the future that they might be scattered, and the very "solution" they invented to prevent this fate actually led to their eventual scattering by the Lord. In the modern vernacular, this would qualify as an epic fail.

I want to highlight a very important statement by the Lord in Genesis 11:6. He implies that if these pagan men on the plain of Shinar continue to speak the same language (enabling their cooperation), then "nothing they plan to do will be impossible for them." This has profound implications for the power of cooperation, let alone unity, among the sons of God. The pagans in Shinar did not have the power of the Holy Spirit to draw from; yet they were deemed capable by the Lord of doing anything they planned to do. This principle is not generally recognized, although there is an understanding of the power of multiplication or synergy during cooperative ventures.

The Lord's statement of the incredible potential of cooperative men goes far beyond what we might currently imagine for the possibilities of human endeavor and presumably refers to the immense creativity and ability to implement plans that was given to Adam and his successive generations and perhaps has become more latent than we realize today.[179] Given this ability described by the Lord, imagine if you can the tremendous potential of the sons of God acting in unity and empowered by the Holy Spirit! Surely, "everything is possible for him who believes."[180] If our motivation is birthed from our place in the heart of Abba, then there will be amazing demonstrations of His desire to "show Himself strong" on our behalf.[181]

Creativity Is Eternal

Given that the joy of expressing our imaginations through creative action is a huge blessing from Abba, it is not likely that He will take it away when we join Him in heaven forever. In fact, I believe that we will be cocreating with Abba for eternity. It is part of Adam's destiny (and *ours*) to create. We were originally (in Adam) on track to live forever with Abba, creating to our heart's delight with His help and guidance as a loving Father. Now that Jesus has restored all things,

---

179. We *do* have some modern examples of outrageous capability, such as successfully visiting the moon and probing the depths of the universe or sub-nuclear particles with fantastic instruments.

180. See Mark 9:23.

181. See 2 Chronicles 16:9a.

we are again "on track" to live forever with Abba, delighting in our joint ventures of creativity and anticipating an unlimited number of possible (and eventual) expressions of love for one another.

As I meditate on the possibilities (a limited meditation at best) of the expressions of our creativity in partnership with Abba in heaven for eternity, I usually find my mind reeling from the sheer magnitude of what I can imagine, let alone what Abba can dream. We can all be encouraged to dream big now for the possible outworking of our creativity in a variety of genres, but "big" in this context is infinitesimally small compared to what we shall progressively discover in eternity with Abba. This is indicated by His infinite love for us and His concomitant desire to see us experience fantastic joy in tasting the fruit of our creativity. When we really begin to realize what is in store for us, then we can begin to understand why Abba's plans[182] for us are such a treasure to Him.

"Time" Will Cease to Have "Value"

Our joy in creative expression here on earth is truly a smidgeon, a taste of what is to come. With unlimited power and resources in heaven available to us, we will be free to let our imaginations soar in the way that Abba intended for Adam's family. We will partake in His divine nature with increasing awareness that everything is possible, and we will shed the limitations that seemed so dominant during our earthly walks. Not only will there be incredible freedom to avail ourselves of the limitless power and resources provided by Abba, but there is another fantastically powerful freedom that will impact our creative destinies in heaven in ways that will be joyfully, and progressively, realized through experience.

Namely, we won't be in any rush to "finish" our creative works, at least in the same way that we are now constrained by earthly time frames. We will have all the time we need to imagine, plan, craft the ideas, implement the fashioning processes, fine-tune the resulting

---

182. See Jeremiah 29:11; see also the discussion in the chapter entitled The Window of the Future.

masterpieces, deliver them to their intended recipients, and then have "no less time" to do the next thing on our list. That is the nature of eternity—no matter how much time has passed, there is no less ahead of us. This is why time will cease to have value in the traditional sense. It will be impossible to use it up or feel pressure to finish our personal projects rapidly. Imaginations will be truly free to soar, much as a caged animal can freely explore his vastly expanded domain upon release from the cage.

For example, if I want to, say, compose a symphony a billion years from now, then I will still have all the time I needed to do so. If I don't know how to read music, I can learn. I can even create new instruments, craft them, learn to play them, record sound tracks for each one, do the same for all the other instruments written into my score, and then mix them all to produce the symphonic masterpiece I envisioned a billion years before. Once completed, I can then offer the recorded CD to Abba as a gift of affection. And I know He will display it on His "fridge."

How Big Is Your Fridge, Abba?

I often imagine that Abba posts your works of art on His heavenly "fridge" for all to see.[183] His joy as a result of our creations is incredible and perhaps infinitely more so into eternity as your creativity matures and expands without any limitation. He will encourage all the heavenly host to take a look at your newest creation, and He will be blessed in the creativity of every one of His sons and daughters as they repeatedly bring their masterpieces to Him, perhaps to just enjoy His smile as He lovingly receives them and places them on the fridge.

I believe that you will not only be creating amazing things for Abba, but also for all the other children of God in heaven. That will take a while, as you make something for each saint, but so what? There is no shortage of time to continue being creative and rejoice in the process of expressing your love for each of your brothers and

---

183. See the chapter entitled The Window of Pride.

sisters. Once you have finished any of your creative projects, you will have just as much time left to do another, and another, and on and on.

Abba's gift of eternity, and its impact on your joy of creating, is underexplored and always will be.

The Window of Joy

"Father, what is Your favorite emotion?"

There is a challenge in encapsulating the window of joy into just one chapter because Abba's joy is boundless and pervasive in its presence all through His infinite heart. You may already have the sense that this indescribable joy of the Father is at the core of much of what you've read so far. It is reasonable to conclude that every perspective includes joy in Abba's heart when looking through a variety of windows. Perhaps it is even his "favorite" emotion. At the very core of Abba's emotions is love, of course, but the joy that springs from His love for us is itself beyond description.

Nevertheless, Abba earnestly desires for us to share in His joy and not just examine it, as one might be content to do when studying a microbe through a microscope. This desire was explicitly expressed by Jesus when He strongly encouraged His disciples to stay connected to Him (i.e., dwell in Him) and, in so doing, experience incredible joy:

> *I have told you these things so that My joy and delight may be in you, and that your joy may be made full and complete and overflowing* (John 15:11 AMP).

In the parable of the talents, Jesus encourages His disciples regarding one of the rewards that await our faithful stewardship of those things that are entrusted[184] to us by Abba (and His Son)—namely, the invitation to share in His joy:

---

184. See the chapter entitled The Window of Trust.

Windows to the Father's Heart

His master said to him, "Well done, good and faithful servant. You have been faithful and trustworthy over a little, I will put you in charge of many things; share in the joy of your master" (Matthew 25:21 AMP).

As recorded by Jude, Abba is able to do something quite remarkable:

Now to Him who is able to keep you from stumbling or falling into sin, and to present you unblemished [blameless and faultless] in the presence of His glory with triumphant joy and unspeakable delight (Jude 24 AMP).

Peter also declares a wonderful blessing of faith in Christ:

Though you have not seen Him, you love Him; and though you do not even see Him now, you believe and trust in Him and you greatly rejoice and delight with inexpressible and glorious joy (1 Peter 1:8 AMP).

From these Scriptures, and many others, we see that our joy is so huge that it is "overflowing," "unspeakable," "inexpressible," and so on. This superabundance of joy that keeps growing even beyond what we think we can hold is cause for yet more joy in the heart of Abba. As we have shared already in other chapters, Abba's blessing because of our blessing is a delightful consequence of His love for us. Somehow, we can bless our Father by simply receiving the joy He has purposed for us. And the process of divine escalation of blessing continues into eternity with Abba, with never-ending mutual enhancement of blessing through our relationships with Him and with each other.

Behold, how good and how pleasant it is for brothers to dwell together in unity! It is like the precious oil [of consecration] poured on the head, coming down on the beard, even the beard of Aaron, coming down upon the edge of his [priestly] robes [consecrating the whole body]. It is like the dew of [Mount] Hermon coming down

142

The Window of Joy

*on the hills of Zion; for there the Lord has commanded
the blessing: life forevermore* (Psalms 133:1-3 AMP).

Returning to the question of how Abba regards the blessings
He has purposed for us, there is undoubtedly an infinite list of such
blessings. Yet, it is instructive to at least consider some representative
blessings for us, and for Abba, that are clear (or at least implied) from
the window perspectives we have introduced in this volume.[185] These
are summarized in the table below:

Window	Our Blessing(s) Knowing...	Reasons(s) for Abba's Joy
Value	Our importance to Abba	Our acceptance of His opinion
Adoption	Our place in Abba's heart	Our acceptance of sonship
Pride	What Abba thinks of us	Thrill of boasting about His children
Pleasure	How we please Abba	Our choices to believe Him
Choice	Abba's sacrifice to give us free will	Our ability to make good choices
The Future	Unlimited potential	Our future is a part of Him
Eternity	Ever-increasing revelation of love	No end to our increasing blessing
Trust	Exquisite affirmation	Our confidence because of His trust
Support	Unlimited resource/power	Our reception of His help
Affection	Daily "kisses" from Abba	Showering love on us every day
Generations	Accumulated wisdom/ knowledge	Mutual blessings among generations
Curiosity	Thrill of discovery	Our delight in learning
Turning	Mending of family relationships	Our hearts being blessed
Creativity	Expanded imagination	Our sharing in His delight of creating
Joy	Ultimate shared pleasure with Abba	Our joy becoming complete

185. If the Lord permits, there may be additional volumes forthcoming that describe other
windows to the Father's heart. There are a huge (an *infinite)* number of them.

True Freedom

As you consider even a few of the ways in which Abba experiences incredible joy because of *you*, it surely must be difficult to continue to entertain thoughts of unworthiness, insignificance, orphanage,[186] futility, loneliness, helplessness, sadness, and so on. Such thoughts begin to diminish and fade away altogether as the Truth does His work:

> *So Jesus was saying to the Jews who had believed Him, "If you abide in My word [continually obeying My teachings and living in accordance with them, then] you are truly My disciples. And you will know the truth [regarding salvation], and the truth will set you free [from the penalty of sin]"* (John 8:31-32 AMP).

Because Jesus has taught and demonstrated the love of the Father, all believers have the opportunity to be set free from thoughts such as those outlined above. We need to embrace the teachings of Jesus, allowing them to shape a lifestyle of obedience that bears the fruit of knowledge of the truth. Wonderful freedom accompanies the victories over the schemes of the enemy that threaten to trap us in the viperous nest of lies evidenced by thoughts like those listed above.

Such glorious freedom is not limited to a mere escape from negativity, however. Abba desires *much* more for us and has been intent on tremendously blessing His children from *before* the beginning. Freedom from entrapments would not have been an issue at all if it weren't for sin entering the world through Adam and Eve. The joy intended for us by Abba in the beginning was not based on freedom from sin. That freedom, purchased for us by Jesus' sacrifice, is essential to *recover* right relationship with Abba so that we can then move on to experience the incredible joy He originally purposed for us.

The process of shedding the shackles of negativity will become a distant memory as we delightfully pursue (and receive) the ever-increasing joy that accompanies the ever-growing relationship with

---

186. The state of being an orphan.

The Window of Joy

Abba that is a hallmark of true freedom. Such release from the wicked hindrances that may have beset us is part of the progression of freedom that began with salvation. Initial freedom from slavery to the Devil forms the basis for subsequent freedom from our own patterns of negative, deceptive self-regard. In fact:

> *So if the Son sets you free, you will be free indeed* (John 8:36).

> *It is for freedom that Christ has set us free* (Galatians 5:1a).

Because we have been set free to experience the true, complete freedom that Abba designed for us from the beginning, we can experience the true joy that comes with our inheritance of the kingdom. There is a presentation coming in which we will stand before "the presence of His glory with triumphant joy and unspeakable delight."[187]

It is interesting to note that our freedom to fully enjoy our relationship with Abba would be a concept quite foreign to us if sin had not entered the earth through Adam and Eve. How could we be aware of freedom if there had never been bondage? Freedom as a concept would essentially be limited to an understanding of God's declaration of freedom to eat of any tree in the garden of Eden except the Tree of the Knowledge of Good and Evil:

> *So the Lord God took the man [He had made] and settled him in the Garden of Eden to cultivate and keep it. And the Lord God commanded the man, saying, "You may freely (unconditionally) eat [the fruit] from every tree of the garden; but [only] from the tree of the knowledge (recognition) of good and evil you shall not eat, otherwise on the day that you eat from it, you shall most certainly die [because of your disobedience]"* (Genesis 2:15-17 AMP).

---

187. See Jude 24 (AMP).

Freedom, therefore, is not an essential prerequisite for joy. Joy can be experienced in the process of obtaining freedom, but freedom once attained through salvation and deliverance is no longer a focus of our thinking but rather a faded concept as we focus on our exquisite relationship with Abba instead. In this sense, true freedom is something that, once attained, is no longer on the radar screen.

If sin had not entered the world, then our present joy would not be dependent on a comparison to sadness. The innocence of the initially pure life of Adam and Eve would necessarily accommodate the purest joy possible. Is it even possible that Adam and Eve would have experienced the joy we know here on earth if they never sinned? That is doubtful because our joy was purchased by Jesus who "for the joy set before him endured the cross"![188] Although we could investigate this question further, it is good to remember that we are made in God's image and that He experienced joy in anticipation of the relationship that we share with Him. His love "compels" Him to share this infinite, relational joy with us, and there will be no need to somehow amplify the intensity of this pure joy through comparison with any of its possible opposites.

Divine Escalation of Joy: Blessing

In much the same way that we concluded that the revelation of Abba's good and infinite love to us demands that eternity exist,[189] we can also conclude that His ever-increasing joy will require eternity to experience. His joy *because* of us will always keep increasing, so the revelation of His joy *to* us will never be finished. As we share in Abba's increasing heart-joy, our own joy also increases because of our love for Him, and this further increases *His* joy because we have been blessed. This is another way to view the never-ending "divine escalation" of blessing[190] between Abba and His children.

---

188. See Hebrews 12:2.

189. See the chapter entitled The Window of Eternity.

190. For examples, see the chapters entitled The Window of Pride, The Window of Pleasure, and The Window of Trust.

The Window of Joy

*The "belly-laughs" of Abba will reverberate through
time and space forever.*

What is the reason for this laughter? *You.*

The first question in the *Westminster Shorter Catechism*[191] is: "What is the chief end of man?" The answer given in the catechism is: "Man's chief end is to glorify God, and to enjoy Him forever." In modern language, we might use *duty* or *purpose* rather than *end.* While there could be, and has been, much debate concerning exactly how to glorify God, the admonishment to "enjoy Him forever" would likely not be strenuously opposed by the majority of the body of Christ.

Our enjoyment of Abba is at the core of His heart because of His incredible love for us. I think a case could be made that to glorify God is, in fact, to enjoy Him, which would render the first phrase of the catechism redundant. Be that as it may, one of the main themes of this book is the interconnectedness of our blessing with Abba's because of our exquisitely entwined relationship with Him. Therefore, it is essential to recognize that our joy is entwined with Abba's joy. As we mature in our relationship with Him, our oneness[192] that develops with Him is evidenced by the increasing mutual sharing of joy, with each other as well as with Abba. In a sense, the maturation of our joy, although continuing to develop forever, is aimed at becoming indistinguishable from Abba's joy. In short,

Abba's joy is becoming yours, and vice versa.

191. Douglas F. Kelly, "The Westminster Shorter Catechism" in John L. Carlson, and David W. Hall, *To Glorify and Enjoy God: A Commemoration of the 350th Anniversary of the Westminster Assembly,* Edinburgh: Banner of Truth Trust, 1994.

192. See John 17:20-23.

The Window of Windows

"Father, what are we looking at?"

In this volume, I have shared a spectrum (but still just an infinitesimal sampling) of possible windows through which to view Abba's heart, with the hope that the reader would be encouraged in a few key ways, including the development of:

(1) Greater personal hope that each of His children can view Abba's heart for themselves,

(2) Increased belief that Abba arranges encounters to openly display His heart,

(3) More belief that Abba derives great joy when His children discover more of His heart,

(4) More boldness to explore Abba's heart, particularly by asking Him questions,

(5) Heightened anticipation of thrilling discoveries of Abba's feelings for His children,

(6) Increased willingness to learn about Abba's heart through experiences as well as His Word, and

(7) Expanded desire to share discovered treasures in Abba's heart with others who need to know Him better (that would be *everyone*).

Windows to the Father's Heart

A Confession

I have a confession to make. I've presented the material in such a way as to fortify the impression that we've been looking through windows *into* the Father's heart from the perspective of an *outsider* looking in, as would a prospective house hunter who looks into a locked house through various windows to get an appreciation of the interior. But *this* "house" is already our *home*. If we have been adopted into His family, we now live *inside* Abba's heart. We are not foreigners trying to get a glimpse of the interior but royal children living *inside* the mansion of His heart because of our "re-birthright."

In a sense, we have been looking through these several windows from the *inside* outward. In a very powerful way, we have been invited by Abba to "see" as He does. When He invites us to discover a certain aspect of His heart, He wants us to experience and share in the joy He has because of us and to gain a perspective of our brothers and sisters in Christ that is more like His each time we look "through a window." Abba's desire is that we learn to love as He loves, and what better way is there to help us in that development than to share His vantage point with us?

I believed during my writing that this perspective "revelation" could perhaps be better appreciated at the end of the book, rather than trying to build a platform at the beginning for a viewing place "inside" Abba's heart. But now that the ideas have had time to brew a bit, I think the delight you may be experiencing is probably worth the reversal of perspectives at this pause in your discoveries. I use the word *pause* because I happily believe that you will rather quickly begin (or *resume*) finding your own windows through which to discover more of Abba's heart. I encourage you to reread some (or all) of the chapters with a fresh posture or positioning *inside* Abba's heart, with a heightened sense that you really are becoming one with Him, as Jesus so earnestly desired.[193]

To be sure, *both* perspectives are valuable, from the outside inward or from the inside outward, because we live in both places simultaneously.

---

193. See, for example, Jesus' prayer recorded in the John 17.

This is part of the mystery of Abba's immense love and causes many a brain to fry, so to speak. But topological correctness is not the goal. A better understanding of the intense love that fashioned us and invites us to share in immeasurable joy is the goal.

The Window of Windows

Another summary revelation that is important to emphasize now is that every one of the windows though which we have been looking can itself be regarded as a "pane" of a much bigger window, The Window of Windows. All of our windows in this volume have a unifying theme, namely *Love*. The *only* thing we shall ever find in Abba's heart is a derivative of love because He *is* love. We've been viewing Abba's heart of love through various angles or viewpoints, but the common result is a deeper appreciation of how much He loves us.

Because Abba's love is infinite, as we've rehearsed before, The Window of Love is itself infinite, with infinitely many panes, like the few we've described. There is no limit to the number of ways we can choose to view His love. We might somehow be able to parrot Elizabeth Barrett Browning's Sonnet #43, which begins, "How do I love thee? Let me count the ways," as we try to describe how we love Abba. But Abba Himself would never count the ways He loves us because they are *innumerable*.

The Transforming Power of Viewing

There are very real, tangible consequences of viewing Abba's heart. For example, we are *transformed* in the process. Abba's love is transformative and always changes the pliable hearts of His children if they are surrendered to His love. The apostle Paul relies on a similar principle when he admonishes believers to "be transformed by the renewing of your mind."[194] In our present context, it is impossible to be so rigid in the presence of the exceedingly great revelation of Abba's love, delivered to us in a supernatural way via the spirit of revelation, that we can remain unchanged by this love. The power of His love is

---

194. See Romans 12:2.

unmatched by any other force in existence. Indeed, every other force we know of was, at its foundation, birthed by His love for us.[195] Our hearts are made new, in a sense, by the revelation of Abba's heart so that we are transformed at our core in the process.

The various revelations of Abba's love are worked together for your good.[196] Because Abba is infinitely capable and creative, it shouldn't be surprising that you might have difficulty understanding, or even seeing, the intricacies of His handiwork in your transformation processes. Nevertheless, if you don't predicate your belief on your understanding, you will be in the perfect position to receive the exquisite blessing of this never-ending[197] gift of Abba. Let me summarize with an adaptation of Paul's admonishment:

Be transformed by the viewing of His heart.

An Exquisite Elusiveness

Now we come to the realization of an exquisite elusiveness. The more we discover about Abba's heart as we look through additional windows (in any direction), the more windows (panes) we discover. This is another mystery concerning Abba's heart, namely that the remainder of the infinity (His heart) we haven't yet probed seems to itself be multiplied by the little piece we just discovered.

This is truly a frustrating mathematics for those who feel compelled to get a grip on the nature of Abba. May I simply ask, "How's that working for you?" Abba, by His own nature, delights in expanding our awe of Him when we think we have grasped any segment of His nature. His love compels Him to partner with us in the magnification

---

195. Perhaps I have a special delight in this because of my background as a physicist, but there is no less a unique delight that each believer experiences because of their own background which may not have prompted encounters with the word "force" all that often.

196. See Romans 8:28. The "all things" in this verse includes "good things," and Abba's love revelations are certainly good things.

197. The ongoing nature of the revelation of Abba's love is described briefly in the chapter entitled The Window of Eternity.

of His "awesomeness" that we can view or sense in some manner. Not only does the infinity (of His discoverable love) exist, it reveals its own infinitude in an expanded way the more we probe its depths. It is very fitting that in coming to the conclusion of this book, I'm realizing more how much more of Abba's heart I still have to discover.

Far from being a frustration, this elusive quality is actually intended as an exquisite gift from Abba. The holy shock value of this type of revelation will surely cause us to forever keep joining the twenty-four elders in casting down our crowns at the feet of the Holy One, only to pick them up again when we are ready for more shock and awe.

The Most Fascinating Place in the Universe

Because of my training and experience as a physicist, I am familiar with the escalating fascination provided by one discovery after another of God's handiwork in the universe, at the extremes of very large sizes of super-galactic objects and incredibly small distances of subnuclear interactions between "elementary" particles and everywhere in between. My fascination level goes off the charts when pondering these creations of Abba, and of course I'm not alone in such ecstasy because all of His children are in awe of the splendor of His creation.

As fascinating as these creations are, there is a place that is yet far more fascinating—Abba's heart itself. His heart *contains* all of creation even as He is present in all of it. But the love that is the essence of His being (His heart) is beyond all the rest of the possible fascinations we may have. Christ is its embodiment. It is the reason for our very existence. It is the reason for the existence of everything else. It is the motivation for everything Abba does for us and through us.

For these reasons, and many others like them, we are, at the same time, the subjects of Paul's prayer for all believers *as well as* co-pray-ers on behalf of our brothers and sisters:

> *I keep asking that the God of our Lord Jesus Christ,*
> *the glorious Father, may give you the Spirit of*

wisdom and revelation, so that you may know him better (Ephesians 1:17).

I believe with all my heart that you, my beloved reader who has reached this concluding chapter, are experiencing deeper treasures in Abba's heart because of Paul's prayer and mine. And that is because Abba has been listening to your cry as well as mine:

"Daddy, show me more of Your heart."

May you continue to know His heart better, and better, and better, and...

Amen.

154

About the Author

In the mid-1990s, Steve Trullinger traded his secure, tenured position as a physics professor at the University of Southern California for a faith walk of adventure, trusting in the Lord's design for the second half of his life. His twenty-five years as an educator helped prepare him to train evangelistic mission teams that have led several tens of thousands to Christ and brought the Father's healing touch to many thousands in East Africa. One of Steve's favorite pastimes is to help his team members get "wrecked beyond recognition!"

Late in 2000, Steve founded The Father's Touch Ministries and now travels extensively around the world to release encouragement among the sons of God, to help them step into their destiny, and to please God by exercising faith in His promises. He also supports and equips his spiritual sons and daughters who are themselves spiritual parents to many. This inter-generational family provides training and encouragement to many leaders in the Body of Christ, especially in East Africa.

Steve has four grown children, two grandchildren, and currently resides in Torrance, California.

Steve can be contacted by email at: steve@fatherstouch.org.

We are a Christian-based publishing company that was founded in 2009. Our primary focus has been to establish authors.

"5 Fold Media was the launching partner that I needed to bring *The Transformed Life* into reality. This team worked diligently and with integrity to help me bring my words and vision into manifestation through a book that I am proud of and continues to help people and churches around the world. None of this would have been possible without the partnership and education I received from 5 Fold Media."

- Pastor John Carter, Lead Pastor of Abundant Life Christian Center, Syracuse, NY, Author and Fox News Contributor

*The Transformed Life is foreworded by Pastor A.R. Bernard, received endorsements from best-selling authors Phil Cooke, Rick Renner, and Tony Cooke, and has been featured on television shows such as TBN and local networks

5 Fold Media
315.570.3333 | 5701 E. Circle Dr. #338, Cicero, NY 13039
manuscript@5foldmedia.com

Find us on Facebook, Twitter, and YouTube

Discover more at www.5FoldMedia.com.

157